Gülçin Mutlu • Ali Yıldırım
Research-driven Curriculum Design

Gülçin Mutlu
Ali Yıldırım

Research-driven Curriculum Design
Developing a Language Course

Verlag Barbara Budrich
Opladen • Berlin • Toronto 2021

All rights reserved. No part of this publication may be reproduced, stored in or introduced into a retrieval system, or transmitted, in any form, or by any means (electronic, mechanical, photocopying, recording or otherwise) without the prior written permission of Barbara Budrich Publishers. Any person who does any unauthorized act in relation to this publication may be liable to criminal prosecution and civil claims for damages.

You must not circulate this book in any other binding or cover and you must impose this same condition on any acquirer.

A CIP catalogue record for this book is available from
Die Deutsche Bibliothek (The German Library)

© 2021 by Verlag Barbara Budrich GmbH, Opladen, Berlin & Toronto
www.budrich.eu

 ISBN 978-3-8474-2426-0
 eISBN 978-3-8474-1563-3
 DOI   10.3224/84742426

Das Werk einschließlich aller seiner Teile ist urheberrechtlich geschützt. Jede Verwertung außerhalb der engen Grenzen des Urheberrechtsgesetzes ist ohne Zustimmung des Verlages unzulässig und strafbar. Das gilt insbesondere für Vervielfältigungen, Übersetzungen, Mikroverfilmungen und die Einspeicherung und Verarbeitung in elektronischen Systemen.

Die Deutsche Bibliothek – CIP-Einheitsaufnahme
Ein Titeldatensatz für die Publikation ist bei der Deutschen Bibliothek erhältlich.

Verlag Barbara Budrich GmbH
Stauffenbergstr. 7. D-51379 Leverkusen Opladen, Germany

86 Delma Drive. Toronto, ON M8W 4P6 Canada
www.budrich.eu

Jacket illustration by Bettina Lehfeldt, Kleinmachnow, Germany –
 www.lehfeldtgraphic.de
Typesetting by Anja Borkam, Jena, Germany – kontakt@lektorat-borkam.de

Preface

This book is a study on curriculum design that includes the practices in relation to needs assessment, course development and testing. The aim of the book is to provide the reader with a systematic and research-wise course design primarily in languages and also in other discipline areas. The course design process is a type of research that is to be conducted in several stages by following the academic guidelines in curriculum theory and then reflecting on all this theory during the research-oriented practices. Thus, course design appears to be a process in which curriculum theory is linked to educational research and practice. However, given the currently available books on the market, it appears that there is a need for a source that would include or synthesize theory and practice. That is, there is a lack of available sources that include practical applications of theoretical information on curriculum development in combination with a concrete curriculum and course design process. As most books on course or curriculum design lack a concrete example with all the necessary steps of curriculum design, we believe that this book will fill this gap with its full and detailed explanations as to the necessary steps for course design. Furthermore, this book will meet the above need by emphasizing the course design process as a very important research-driven practice. To serve these ends, we believe that this book will be beneficial for researchers working on educational sciences and foreign languages, as well as for those working as professionals (teachers, lecturers etc.) in the teaching of languages and other discipline areas.

This book is composed of 7 chapters. Chapter 1 serves as an introductory part to the study and to all of the other parts of the book. Chapter 2 provides the literature review for language courses and curriculum design and this part centers around three main dimensions: a) conceptual, b) procedural and c) research-wise background to the language curriculum development. Chapter 3 gives information about the needs assessment, which is the first step in the curriculum design process. Chapter 4 discusses the curriculum design model used in the study and its relevant procedures and more specifically the end product of each particular process determined on the curriculum design model. Chapter 5 provides a unit and a sample lesson plan generated as a result of the curriculum development process told in the previous chapters. Chapter 6 gives information about the field testing of the sample lesson plan provided and mentioned in the previous chapter. Chapter 7 concludes the book with a discussion of final comments on the curriculum development process and with the inclusion of some recommendations for future developmental studies in this area. We believe that the procedures and tactics related to course design and development given in this source will be beneficial for those aiming to design their own courses by utilizing the theoretical and practical information provided in this book.

Dr. Gülçin Mutlu & Dr. Ali Yıldırım

* Preliminary results of the study reported in this book was presented at the European Research Conference (EERA- *ECER 2017 Copenhagen: Reforming Education and the Imperative of Constant Change: Ambivalent roles of policy and educational research*) in 2017 in Copenhag, Denmark.

Table of Contents

1. Introduction 11
2. Review of Literature 13
   2.1 Conceptual Background: Theoretical Influence on the Basis of Language Curriculum 13
       2.1.1 Acquisition-learning distinction 14
       2.1.2 Comprehensible input 15
       2.1.3 Affective filter 16
       2.1.4 Competence and performance in language 17
       2.1.5 Nature of linguistic communication 18
   2.2 Design and Procedural Background: Communicative Curriculum in Theory and Practice 18
       2.2.1 Nature of language 18
       2.2.2 Nature of language learning 19
       2.2.3 Nature of educational-cultural philosophy 20
   2.3 Research-wise Background: Studies in relation to English Speaking Skills 20
   2.4 Authentic Materials and Communicative Competence 23
3. Needs Assessment 25
   3.1 A Snapshot of the Needs Assessment 25
       3.1.1 Who Were Involved in the Needs Assessment? 25
       3.1.2 What Types of Information Was Gathered? (Present Situation Analysis and Target Situation Analyses) 26
       3.1.3 How Was This Information Gathered? 26
   3.2 Needs Assessment Plan for the Further Speaking Course 27
       3.2.1 Data collection procedures 27
       3.2.2 Data analysis procedures 29
       3.2.3 Results of the needs assessment 29
   3.3 Reflections from the Needs Assessment to Use in the Design of the Further Speaking Skills Curriculum 38

4.	Curriculum Design	41
	4.1 Description and Components of the Curriculum Design Model Used	41
	4.2 Application of the Model to the Further Speaking Course	46
	4.2.1 Articulating beliefs	46
	4.2.2 Defining the context and needs assessment	47
	4.2.3 Formulating goals and rationale	48
	4.2.4 Conceptualizing content and course grid	49
	4.2.5 Organizing the course and course syllabus	52
	4.2.6 Refined course goals and intended learning outcomes	53
	4.2.7 Instructional planning and an instructional plan for the FSC	59
	4.2.8 Methods (teaching) strategies	59
	4.2.9 Planning Evaluation and an Evaluation Plan for the FSC	62
5.	Unit and Lesson Plan	65
	5.1 Unit Plan	65
	5.1.1 Rationale	65
	5.1.2 Introduction	65
	5.1.3 Sequence	66
	5.1.4 Instructional foci	66
	5.1.5 ILOs	66
	5.1.6 General teaching strategies	67
	5.1.7 Unintended learning outcomes	67
	5.1.8 Evaluation	68
	5.2 Lesson Plan	68
6.	Field Testing of the Unit Plan	71
7.	Discussion	76
	7.1 Comments on the Process and Design	76
	7.2 Suggestions for Further Course Design Work	79
References		81

Appendices 83
    Appendix A 83
    Appendix B 84
    Appendix C 85
    Appendix D 86
    Appendix E 87
    Appendix F 88
    Appendix G 92
    Appendix H 93
    Appendix I 94
    Appendix J 95
Index 99

1. Introduction

The purpose of the study reported in this book is to develop an advanced level speaking course that will be offered to the freshman students successfully completing the English preparatory program, which was composed of more than 700 hours of English instruction. This target population of students spends their first year of university at the preparatory English school and they have to successfully complete the preparatory school before they start their main faculties. The students at all preparatory classes usually start with the elementary level of proficiency, and they are expected to move towards an upper level of proficiency level within a whole academic year and finally graduate with an upper intermediate to advanced levels of proficiencies. The students are usually aged between 18 and 20 at the preparatory class, and thus for the year that this speaking course is to be offered, students are expected to be generally aged between 19 and 21. To our experience at several universities in Turkey, these students start university after having been exposed to a highly traditional high school period and school culture. That is, they are accustomed to seeing the teacher as an authority as a figure who always provides them with step-by-step explanations of what they are going to do in class. Given the interactional patterns in the classrooms, based upon their earlier experiences at the high schools, they are not very attentive and willing to work with others for their classroom tasks. However, as they spend a relatively more time in the language classroom, they are observed to change their attitudes to a great extend in comparison to their first weeks and behave in a more relaxed and cooperative manner in the classrooms. Therefore, when they come to the advanced speaking course to be designed for the purposes of this study, they are expected to be already accustomed to a cooperative classroom environment, to teachers behaving like a theater director and guide (not like an authority) and treating the students as active course participants. The course to be designed was named as "Further Speaking Course" (FSC) as the main purpose of this course to make students further their speaking abilities that they have already developed a certain level at the preparatory classes. Hence, this course is built upon the understanding that the target students have a certain level of proficiency in English with regard to language forms, lexical knowledge, use of conversational strategies and registers in communication, and certain level of writing and speaking skills in English.

Given the contextual characteristics, the medium of instruction at the university where we designed this course was Turkish in general. However, the courses are offered with the medium of English on a partial basis in some of the departments and the preperatory class is compulsory for these departments. That is, for some departments, the students study 30 % of the courses in their faculty curriculum in English. The course we attempted to design in this project will be offered to those departments that offer their degree curricula partially in English (i.e. with 30 % of English instruction). This course to be designed in this study will be offered as an elective course for those students who want to further develop their speaking skills. However, in the long run, there may be some departments at the university that will offer all of the degree courses with the medium of English, and in this case, the course to be designed can be offered as a must course. The Further Speaking Skills course will meet for four hours a week in the fall term of an academic year when the students start their degree studies upon the successful completion of the preparatory school. This makes a period of approximately four months for the course.

The English preparatory program is a strict program in which students receive instruction concerning all of the four major skills (listening, writing reading and speaking) and the three sub-skills (grammar, vocabulary, pronunciation) of language. Though we follow a communicative approach to language teaching with a focus upon all four major language skills at the preperatory class from the very beginning of the preparatory semester, it takes time for students to come to a level of production in language for both oral and written purposes. To our experience, their competence (knowledge about the language) precedes their performance (use of the language). However, once they have gained the necessary competence and input in English, they are expected to proceed very well. In this regard, as researchers and teachers we assume that these students develop their competencies to a great extent at the preparatory program; however, they still need more practice for the productive skills of language (for their performance in English). Accordingly, having completed the preparatory class, these students have the ability to produce language on most parts, but there still remain some areas of speaking (e.g. like making speeches before an audience, producing longer stretches of spoken discourse and reflecting on the interlocutors' opinions) for these students to develop further so that they can be fully competent communicators in English. Hence, the Further Speaking Skills course to be developed for this study will answer to this main need. It is also believed that this course will add to students' proficiency with other language skills in spite of its preliminary specific focus on speaking skills for it is impossible to isolate the skills of a language as supported by today's latest and current language teaching methodology.

2. Review of Literature

2.1 Conceptual Background: Theoretical Influence on the Basis of Language Curriculum

According to Yalden (1987), course design is a procedure to merge already present knowledge concerning language teaching and learning with the new opinions, wishes and outlook into the world brought by language students to the language class. In this regard, language course designers are to have a certain degree of theoretical knowledge and awareness concerning language teaching and learning proposed in the available literature on second language learning and acquisition.

Any change seen in theory has automatically influenced the practice about second or foreign language teaching. For instance, a particular interest on structural linguistics in the past has resulted in the formulation of structure-based courses and lessons (Dubin & Olshtain, 1986). However, with the particular surge of interest concerning socio-cultural views about the nature of language, sociolinguistic issues and communication have started to gain more and more attention over the years. Hence, it was seen that linguistic theory was introduced with a new sociolinguistic component or perspective (Yalden, 1987). The courses based upon structures (i.e. knowledge about the language) have lost their popularity over the courses based upon or including socio-linguistic knowledge in terms of classroom practice. Such changes also influenced the way we define language proficiency. The understanding of language proficieny as the extend of mastery of the lexical, grammatical or phonological structures of language seen in the traditional language teaching approaches left its place to such an understanding of language profiency realized basically as the ability to communicate. That is, it was realized that languages are needed for communication and thus should be learned for communication and this condition requires more than the structural knowledge regarding the language.

Based on the changes in theory mentioned above, it can be concluded that the communication with others should form the main basis of a speaking course to be designed for today's language teaching purposes. Thus, it would be wise to refer to some theoretical issues regarding communicative purposes of language learning. As is also put forth by Yalden (1987), it should be remembered that changes in theoretical issues will in turn bring about some implications for practice and for course design practices, and these changes should be followed and theoretical information should be updated prior to any course design project.

2.1.1 Acquisition-learning distinction

In his theory of second language acquisition, which has been greatly influential upon second language research and teaching for two decades now, Krashen (1981, 1982) talks about the Acquisition-Learning Hypothesis which proposes that there are two distinct and independent ways of second language competence or performance in adults. "The acquired system" and "the learned system" are further defined as these two independent systems of second language performance. The acquired system, or acquisition, is similar to the process children pass through in acquiring their first language. This process is termed as a subconscious process in that acquirers have no conscious awareness of the rules or of the fact that they are learning a language, but they may have a feel for grammaticality (correctness) and they are aware that they are using the language for communication. Meaningful interaction is very important in such a process in which the focus will be on the communicative act and thus on meaning, not on the form. Another perspective to develop competence in a second language is through conscious way of language learning which stands for knowing about a language, that is, its grammar and rules.

Given the links of this hypothesis with the teaching of speaking, Richards (1990) points out that the learning-acquisition distinction that may underpin one's choice of a teaching approach, that is, whether one will teach speaking directly (stands for learning) or indirectly (stands for acquisition). The direct approach involves the teaching of specific microskills, strategies and processes of fluent conversation (Richards, 1990). While practicing conversation and speaking is considered important in this approach, there is this presupposition that form-focused instruction might be needed at some point during the lesson (Slade & Thurnbury, 2006). The indirect approach, however, claims that learners gain speaking competence simply through doing it. In other words, conversational competence is arrived at as a result of taking part in a conversational interaction (Richards, 1990). As is also put forth by Burns (1998, p. 103), there is a focus on "tasks mediated through language, negotiation and sharing of information" in the development of conversational competence. This reference to the role of tasks equates indirect approach with the task-based learning which is in fact based on the communicative approach with its claim that language is acquired by means of communication.

Although explicit instruction might be helpful in learning certain formulaic routines and conversational move types (e.g. ways of opening and closing conversations, turn-taking and back-channeling), there is a scarcity of evidence in favor of the direct teaching of conversation (Slade & Thurnbury, 2006). Moreover, some characteristics of conversation are universal in that they might be transferred from learners' first languages (Brown & Yule, 1983; McCarthy, 1991).

Slade and Thurnbury (2006) have concluded that there is a case for both an indirect and direct approach in the acquisition of conversational competence. Slade and Thurnbury (2006) argue for what they call as indirect approach plus. In this regard, indirect approach to teaching of speaking would entail exposure to conversational input (preferably authentic ones) through which the learners would be able to extract the conversational moves, lexical chunks and formulaic expressions in an unconscious manner, which corresponds to the idea of acquired way of competence. However, there will be instances where teacher presentation of some explicit features and rules would be needed, such as having students identify discourse markers and hesitation devices.

2.1.2 Comprehensible input

The input hypothesis of Krashen's (1981) second language acquisition theory is based on the question of how people acquire languages, and it holds for the acquisition in the acquisition-learning distinction pole. In his theoretical restatement of the acquisition-learning distinction hypothesis, he inquires how people move from i (current level of proficiency) to i+1 (expected level of proficiency). The main claim of the hypothesis is that in order to move from i to i+1, the acquirer is to understand the input that contains i + 1, which is called as the comprehensible input. The understanding process here requires an emphasis on the meaning of the message not on the form of that. To put it differently, people acquire a second language only when the message given is a little beyond their current level of proficiencies. While doing this, people opt to use the available contextual information, their extra-linguistic knowledge and their general knowledge of the world in addition to their linguistic (grammatical) competence (Krashen, 1981, 1982).

Given the further claims of this hypothesis, one implication relates to the fact that speaking fluency is not possible to be taught directly, but this productive ability develops over time. Provision of the comprehensible input is thus the best way to teach speaking (Krashen, 1981). In this regard, people will speak when they are ready to speak and their early speech will not be grammatically accurate. Accuracy will also develop over time as the learners are provided with more comprehensible input. Equating the child's caretaker speech with a comprehensible input source, Krashen (1981) puts forth that input from the caretaker tend to get more complicated as the child gets more mature. Some other researchers also claimed correlations between child's linguistic maturity (proficiency) and input complexity (Cross, 1977; Newport & Gleitman, 1977, as cited in Krashen, 1981).

Krashen (1981) mentions intake (basically the input to be provided to the students) and the necessary characteristics to be qualified as intake, such as meaningfulness, naturality, being communicative and interesting. He believes that it is the natural and communicative input that will provide some i + 1 or other for everyone.

In connecting Krashen's (1981, 1982) ideas to our case of developing a further speaking skills course, it would be wise to first consider the provision of comprehensible input that is beyond students' current level of proficiency so that the students will later and better generate the output, which simply means that they will speak. It would be unwise to expect accuracy in speaking at the very beginning levels of language proficiency, as students should be allowed for some time for their accuracy to develop. Though the students of this further speaking course will not be allowed for a silent period as the hypothesis claims regarding the early speech development of the children (or second language learners here), students will already possess a particular degree of syntactic competence to express their ideas and opinions because of the course. However, engagement with the materials (receptive skill materials) to be provided as inputs might be thought as such a period for they allocate some time for students to produce speaking and meanwhile they will feel better and more ready for the output, that is, speaking. For the input complexity, it seems logical to provide the learners with more complicated inputs as these students are considered to have made a certain progress towards their English proficiency. Furthermore, given this issue, Krashen (1981) already mentioned a correlation or a compliance between input complexity and learners' proficiency. His suggested criterion for the intake reminds us of the use of authentic materials which are thought to be beyond the level of the students. Krashen (1981) has also mentioned that the intake should be natural to the learners, which in turn may imply that natural and real-like materials should be preferred for the students.

2.1.3 Affective filter

Krashen (1981) claims that even though you provide an input that meets the criteria for the potential good intake, it cannot reach to the language acquisition device in our brain because of some other lacks, such as lack of motivation or positive attitude towards a task. In other words, there is a high affective wall that filters out the input. In this sense, motivational and attitudinal constraints should be satisfied for the linguistic and learning conditions to take place. When the affective filter is high, the acquisition on the part of the learners will be at a very poor level or none even if you provide a good quality, meaningful, communicative and natural input. This claim is termed as affective filter hypothesis, and the implication of this hypothesis for the speaking class to be designed would refer to our creating a relaxing, motivating and enjoyable atmosphere for the learners so that they can make it to the processing of comprehensible input.

2.1.4 Competence and performance in language

Chomsky (1965) differentiated between linguistic competence and linguistic performance. He defined linguistic theory as mentalistic or related to the discovery of mental reality underlying actual behavior. His view showed a drastic opposition to the behaviorist theories of linguistics, which study physical verbal behavior that can be directly seen. Chomsky (1965) characterized linguistic competence as *what a speaker knows* and thus what a linguist is required to work on. As for the linguistic performance, it has been defined as *"what a speaker does (says or writes)"* (Yalden, 1987, p.15), and he suggested that this should not be a concern for the linguist. Hymes (1972), opposing the view of Chomsky (1965), pointed out that Chomsky's category of competence (linguistic) is not related to language use in any way. Moreover, he also asserted that Chomsky's category of performance only deals with the psychological constraints on performance and excludes the concept of social interaction and appropriateness of "what we say or write" (p. 16) in a social context. Hence, Hymes (1972) proposed a need for a new theory of language that will deal with the issues lacking in Chomsky's theoratical conceptualization of competence and performance. Such a new theory should inevitably include interactional competence, and this was later termed as *communicative competence* in the literature. Hymes (1972) believed that it would be a theory of language users and language use. The course to be designed for the purposes of this study reported in this book is a course oriented towards speaking, which is a major productive skill of language and thus it is concerned with the use of language. Therefore, it seems logical to take the theory of communicative competence as the basis for this course to be designed and gain insights from the implications of this theory for language teaching.

Chomsky (1965) believes that the knowledge of language (rules of grammar) absorbed in the mind of the speaker provides the basis for the actual use of the language. Thus, according to Chomsky (1965), this grammaticality is seen as language competence, or in clear terms, as the sign for language proficiency. However, Hymes (1972) has proposed that grammaticality is one of the components of the concept of communicative competence, but communicative competence is much broader. Hymes (1972) identified four kinds of judgments speakers make as they speak or write, which may be considered as the components of communicative competence. These judgments are depending on whether something is "possible (given the forms of expression), feasible (given the means of implementation), appropriate in relation to context and actually performed."

2.1.5. Nature of linguistic communication

Canale and Swain (1980) enlarging the conceptualization suggested by Hymes ((1972) developed a conceptual scheme based on the sociolinguistic view of language within which it would be easier to look at the relationship between theory (linguistics) and practice (language education). The researchers based their conceptual scheme upon the concept of linguistic communication and Canale (1983, p. 3-4) asserts that linguistic communication is

> "a) a form of social interaction, is therefore normally acquired and used in social interaction, b) involves a high degree of unpredictability and creativity in form and message, c) takes place in discourse and socio-cultural contexts which provide constraints on appropriate language use and also clues as to correct interpretations of utterances, d) is carried out under limiting psychological and other conditions, such as memory constraints, fatigue and other distractions, e) always has a purpose (e.g. to establish social relations, to persuade), f) involves authentic, as opposed to text-book contrived language, and g) is judged as successful or not on the basis of actual outcomes."

Based on this conceptualization of linguistic communication, Canale and Swain (1980) mentioned three components of the communicative competence, which later Canale (1983, p. 4) reorganized into a total of four components as "grammatical competence, sociolinguistic competence, discourse competence, and strategic competence". These four components compose the subsystems of one's general language proficiency.

2.2 Design and Procedural Background: Communicative Curriculum in Theory and Practice

Dubin and Olshtain (1986) defines a communicative curriculum as a sort of curriculum centering upon three major sources as a) a sociolinguistic language view, b) a cognitively-based language learning view and c) a humanistic view in terms of educational processes. The following provides more discussion on these views.

2.2.1 Nature of language

An outlook on language as being inseparable from its social context is the theoretical base for a communicative curriculum. In this regard, communicative competence encompasses knowledge of "what to say, when, how, where and to whom" (Dubin & Olshtain, 1986, p. 70). It is apparent from this definition that knowing the language form is not of sole importance, the knowledge of what to say to whom and how to say it appropriately is considered more important in terms of a communicative orientation to language.

2.2.2 Nature of language learning

The basic premise of this view is that learners should be exposed to a variety of cognitive activities, as there is a variety of individual learner styles. This view accepts the existence of general styles, that is, cognitive mechanisms employed by all people, but there is a truth that individual learners develop their own strategies to accomplish a task. Depending on the surge of interest in individual learning tactics with recent discussions in cognitive psychology and information processing models, it is wise to recommend that language learning should include an awareness of these tactics (i.e. learners' own tactics and also the other individuals' tactics; Dubin & Olshtain, 1986). Titone (1981, as cited in Dubin & Olshtain, 1986) supports a holistic approach to learning. He claims that language learning that centers on meaning and communication also encompasses motivation, creativity and self-expression and a focus on individual characteristics of learners in addition to cognitive processes. Communicative thinking about language learning also considers students' errors as valuable part of the language learning process, which drastically conflicts with a behaviorist orientation to learning. Given the nature of language learning in the communicative curriculum, the distinction between context-embedded and context-reduced communication is an important one. In context-embedded communication, participants actively negotiate meaning by relying on the non-linguistic characteristics in the context, while they need to rely mostly on their linguistic repertoire in context reducing situations to understand the meaning. Another important distinction refers to the efforts demanded by the tasks that range from those involving little cognitive demand to those with a lot of cognitive involvement. The most difficult situations for learning to take place are those requiring learners to be engaged with context-reduced communication with cognitively demanding tasks (Cummins, 1981, as cited in Dubin & Olshtain, 1986).

The above discussion regarding negotiation of meaning (learning) and Cummins' (1981, as cited in Dubin & Olshtain, 1986) ideas brings about some implications for foreign language course design and materials development (Dubin & Olshtain, 1986). To begin with, the amount of cognitive demand and involvement required from the learners should be considered in designing learning tasks, and tasks should follow a route from less to more demanding. Second, activities prepared for communication purposes (communicative tasks) should be graded from context-embedded to context-reduced so that students can find time to develop the required skills to manage the context-reduced communication. Another point to consider in course development relates to the content of the courses. That is, the course work should include both accuracy (focus on form) that brings about a better cognitive proficiency and fluency (focus on meaning), which brings about more interaction and developed interpersonal communicative strategies.

2.2.3 Nature of educational-cultural philosophy

A communicative curriculum draws from a humanistic view of education. That is, it attempts to link subject matter to be taught to learners' needs and lives. In this context, the communicative curriculum with its humanistic tone is very similar to the idea of a humanistic curriculum in that learners are always at the forefront. Indivduals take the responsibility of their own learning. They are active in decision-making practices, choose and initiate activities, and freely share their opinions (Dubin & Olshtain, 1986). The following presents some implications of this humanistic view on education for the purposes of language teaching and learning (Dubin & Olshtain, 1986, p. 76):

- Meaningful communication is a priority, and therefore the materials used need to be authentic, tasks to be communicative and outcomes to be negotiated and not predetermined
- Learners are of great importance, and respect for the individual is the key idea.
- Other learners are viewed as supportive peers and all peers interact with, evaluate and help each other.
- The teacher is the facilitator and has a close eye on the class atmosphere.

2.3 Research-wise Background: Studies in relation to English Speaking Skills

In his attempt to develop a speaking curriculum for Chinese two-year-college students, Hongyan (n.d.) first conducted a needs assessment through which he collected students' needs information on the basic components of a curriculum, that is, goals and objectives, language materials, language methods and language tests. Using the data from the needs assessment, he formulated three main goals for the speaking course as a) using everyday language fluently, b) building confidence and lastly c) making conversations and giving a report on something academic. In relation to the content and materials to be employed, he decided to use authentic materials. Though students complained about the difficulty of the authentic materials in the needs assessment study, they also found it childish to work with simplified materials. For the teaching methods, he decided to follow communicative language teaching with a focus on real-life tasks, pair work and group work.

Another attempt to design an advanced English speaking course was performed by Bawcom (1995). Based on the needs assessment study performed with the students and the teachers, she decided to organize a course that followed a communicative orientation to language teaching. To provide the main material for the course, she used *The Reader's Guide to Periodicals* known as the reference book for journal and magazine articles written on specific topics. Thus, it was apparent that she appreciated the use of authentic materials as the input in her speaking course. In her review of literature with the methods to use in this course, she prepared a list of activities (e.g. roleplays, debates; see Appendix A for the list of activities), which again confirms her preference for the communicative approach to language teaching.

Another benefical piece of evidence for the purposes of this study was provided by Jiayan and Jianbin (2010), who compared two English curricula (that were recognized as communicative curricula in China) for their compliance with the communicative competence development of the learners. On the first phase of their research, they did a document analysis of the two curricula concerning the objectives they had. They examined the objectives related to linguistic competence (listening and speaking were considered only), affection and attitudes, cultural awareness and lastly communication strategies in both types of curricula. The results from the document analysis revealed that both types of curricula centered on the communicative competence development. However, one of them was better than the other and thus they recommended the necessary improvement procedures for this good one. The following presents the objectives of these two curricula that are believed to develop communicative competence of the learners (Jiayan & Jianbin, 2010, p.77). Since not all the objectives were well-defined and worded with clarity, only those that made more sense were selected for the purposes of this study and reported in the following part (below follows from objectives for listening to the objectives for speaking, cultural awareness and communication strategies). In this regard, we compiled the following skills based on Jiayan and Jianbin's (2010) analyses. Hence, the students of the FSC to be designed should be able to:

- grasp main ideas and key words in the listening input.
- use basic listening strategies to enhance comprehension.
- understand the various types of listening input (discussions, speeches, debates etc.).
- understand view and purposes of the speaker in longer stretches of speech.
- evaluate the views of others she/he hears.
- talk about hot topics and give opinions.
- give a prepared speech and answer the questions posed about it.
- perform interviews in English.

- explain misunderstandings stemming from miscommunication.
- take part in discussions on the assigned topic.
- show basically correct pronunciation and intonation.
- employ basic conversational strategies in communication and dialogues.
- understand common English idioms and their cultural connotations.
- learn the culture of other countries around the world through English learning.
- deepen their understanding of their own culture through comparing it with other cultures.
- take the initiative in communicating with others in English.
- manage communication in English better by using non-verbal expressions.
- continue the conversations they have started.
- show enthusiasm and interest in English learning.
- demonstrate confidence and courage to communicate in English.
- appreciate cooperation and working with others in learning English.

Erozan's (2005) evaluation case study suggested some useful insights for the purposes of this study. Erozan (2005) performed a curriculum evaluation study of 10 language improvement courses including a course called oral communication skills at an undergraduate teacher education program. Her evaluation results revealed some implications for the oral communication course in terms of course objectives, course implementation, course content and materials and the assessment procedures used, which also could be employed for the purposes of current speaking skills course to be designed. To begin with the course objectives, it was seen that students requested more practice with listening and speaking as one of the course goals. They also suggested presentation skills, discussion skills, taking part in natural conversations and argumentation skills to be emphasized among the goals of the course. For the course content and materials, provision of more input in listening and more opportunities to practice speaking have been emphasized. For the course implementation and teaching-learning process, the use of a variety of methods and activities was stressed in the study. The students also recommended that in-class performance should be included in the final assessment of the students.

Yel (2009) evaluated the English curricula for all grades at a Turkish Anatolian high school that was said to be following a communicative orientation to teaching. The results of her evaluation revealed that students' needs that were related to reading and writing skills were met more than their listening and speaking needs, which was also reflected in the dissatisfaction of the students with the listening and speaking materials. In talking about the implications with regard to the teaching of speaking for future studies, the major suggestion was about the course content and materials. Based on the results, it was reported that the course content should be in line with the goals and approaches of the curriculum, and learners should be exposed to different and varied reading and oral materials. Another suggestion was about the practice opportunities for speaking. The researchers recommended that more practice opportunities should be provided to the students via communicative tasks and activities.

From the above account, it is evident that a speaking course design should draw from such aspects as building confidence (affective goals), development of speaking ability with the help of other language skills, development of ability to perform speeches before an audience, the use of real-life materials and push for intelligible pronunciation. For the teaching of speaking skills, communicative language teaching might be an appropriate approach to follow based on the assumption that language is communication and communication is language in the speaking classes. Moreover, it would be wise to conclude that practice is the key to success and should be an aim of a speaking course so that students will be able to develop and improve their speaking skills. On the way to achieve this aim, the materials to be used are important, and a special care should be given to the materials used in the form of an input for the following speaking practices. These speaking practices should also be provided through communicative tasks and activities.

2.4 Authentic Materials and Communicative Competence

The realization of communicative competence that includes more than the language forms and the realization of the idea of contextualized communication paved the way for the use of authentic materials in language teaching in that they are more effective in providing ideas and opinions rather than the linguistic forms or structures (Gilmore, 2007).

In looking at the foreign language teaching arena, the definition of authenticity is still controversial, elusive and thus devoid of consensus. Guariento and Morley (2001), however, suggest that a general consensus has been reached regarding the fruitful contribution of the use of authentic materials to the learning process. In choosing a relatively better definition among the dozens of definitions available in the literature, the definition put forth by Morrow (1977) makes sense here. According to Morrow (1977, p. 13), "an authentic material is a stretch of real language, produced by a real speaker or writer for a real audience and designed to convey a real message of some sort". From this definition, it is possible to grasp the idea that authenticity lies in the genuiness of a text (Widdowson, 1979), written or spoken. On the other hand, there are some other researchers pointing out that the authenticity is situated in the notion of a task (Nunan, 1988; Guariento & Morley, 2001). For instance, Ellis (1990, p. 195) pointed out the presence of real-life tasks by saying "control over linguistic knowledge is achieved by means of performing under real operating conditions in meaning-focused language activities". Hence, it is appropriate to suggest that in addition to the input—that is, the authentic text—learners need some real operating conditions to produce language. Therefore, not only the texts and but also the tasks within which the texts are put to use should be explored for their authenticity.

From the above explanation, it would be easy to understand that authentic materials have close connections to the development of communicative competence, and they are valuable in providing ideas (input) for the communicative language teaching practices. Whether it is text authenticity, or the authenticity of the tasks organized for classroom practices, authenticity offers a lot for the exploitation of communicative language teaching in the language classrooms.

3. Needs Assessment

3.1 A Snapshot of the Needs Assessment

The researchers began by collecting the necessary information that would form a basis for developing a curriculum that meets the learning needs of the students. Once the researchers learned about the students' needs and expectations, these needs may serve as a basis for the development of other steps (e.g., goals and objectives, testing and materials) of the further speaking skills curriculum. The following section refers to the needs assessment plan designed and employed for the course in question in the light of the recommendations taken from the chapter on needs assessment by Graves' (2000) book in which she discussed the course design framework for foreign language teaching. Before this needs assessment took place, the researchers made some fundamental decisions as to who will be involved in the needs assessment; what types of information should be gathered; how this information will be gathered; and which points of view the researchers should take. (Graves, 2000) and they then gave the necessary answers before beginning the actual needs assessment procedures.

3.1.1 Who Were Involved in the Needs Assessment?

The t*arget group* involved a conveniently reached group of students who completed the English preperatory class last year. The *audience* consisted of course teachers and program administrators at the university where the course would be offered. The students themselves, instructors of English teaching who were experienced in teaching speaking skills and the academicians from students' content courses acted as the *resource group*. Content course teachers were those who were teaching as specialist teachers in such departments as chemistry, physics, engineering and economics. The teachers of the content departments were selected from among those who were feeling close to teaching in English and eager to share their experiences. Once the students complete English preparatory year, the students are required to take 30 % of their courses in English as the medium of instruction in their actual content departments at the faculties. It is also a frequently heard and reported problem by most of these colleagues teaching at these content departments that preparatory program graduates faced problems in communicating with them in English. In this regard, these academicians from the content departments were believed to be a good source of information about the weaknesses of the past years' students in terms of speaking abilities. The needs assessment was conducted by one of the researchers who was also a lecturer of English.

3.1.2 What Types of Information Was Gathered? (Present Situation Analysis and Target Situation Analyses)

Students' wishes and needs were taken into consideration and on the continua of three pairs, a) language needs vs. situation needs, b) objective needs vs. subjective needs and c) linguistic content vs. learning processes (see Graves, 2000 and Nation & Macalister, 2010 for a detailed discussion over the categorizations of needs). At this point, gathering and using information from both parts of each pair was the main concern of the researchers. Learners' linguistic requirements, the observable data about their proficiency and skills levels and the special circumstances were taken into consideration as much as their physical, psychological and social needs. The needs assessment was designed to elicit information related to their *present situation* such as a) learners' language information (current skills and language use), b) learners' personal information, c) learners' linguistic requirements and their lacks, d) the observable data about learners' proficiency and skills levels, e) environmental information and f) the special circumstances and also related to their *target situation* such as a) learners' needs from the course (i.e. future linguistic needs, what's wanted from the course) and b) learners' physical, psychological and social needs.

3.1.3 How Was This Information Gathered?

This was the stage in which the researchers attempted to find out how the information on the present case and future case would be gathered through what instruments. Some other existing programs with similar student populations and their teachers who have taught the same or similar English courses earlier were consulted to gain information concerning the possible topics to include, goals and objectives of the course, teaching-learning process and the course assessment procedures in addition to the literature review about some reliable sources on teaching foreign language speaking courses. The following discusses the needs assessment plan and the relevant procedures performed in detail.

3.2 Needs Assessment Plan for the Further Speaking Course

3.2.1 Data collection procedures

3.2.1.1 A writing activity

Students were invited to set their personal goals and expectations. Students ($n = 10$) were asked to write in Turkish or in English about their past experiences with speaking English, the problems that they have encountered with English, their future needs and expectation from this course and what they hope/want to work on in a speaking class. The students were also asked to specify two goals, which they desired to accomplish during the course (see Appendix B for the activity sheet).

3.2.1.2 Student Interviews

Semi-structured interviews were performed with the students ($n = 6$) who completed the preparatory class last year to elaborate on their ideas they reflected in the writing activity, also on their goals and expectations, preferred ways of course conduct and assessment procedures in this course (see Appendix C for the student interview schedule).

3.2.1.3 Teacher interviews

There were two types of teacher interviews. First, instructors of English language ($n = 3$) who were experienced in teaching of English in general and in teaching of speaking in specific were interviewed. Interviews were open-ended (semi-structured) and centered on eliciting the perceptions of teachers (see Appendix D for the interview schedule for language teachers) in terms of the main components of curriculum development (goals, materials, assessment etc.). Second, academicians ($n = 3$; two associate professors and one professor doctor) from the students' content departments who had experience with prepaeratory program graduate students and who seemed close to teaching in English were interviewed (see Appendix E for the interview schedule for content teachers).

The information gathered from all teacher interviews (language and content teachers) that were further supported also by the insights derived from the writing activity tool were believed to lead to a preliminary determination of topics, activities, skills and tasks relevant to the further speaking skills course to be designed. Interview data elicited regarding speaking skills that would mainly shape the objectives of the course to be designed to a great extend were also used in the formation of the skills part of the student questionnaire.

3.2.1.4 Questionnaires to the students

Student questionnaires were designed to elicit information for the selection of the topics for the course and for the determination of course objectives. The student questionnaire (see Appendix F for the student questionnaire) included two sections. The first section was related to the selection of the topics that would help the researchers shape the course content and the second section was related to the skills that would help the researchers shape the course objectives. On the first section, the students were asked to rate the 15 topics provided for them. For the selection of topics included in the student questionnaire, the researchers consulted *The Reader's Guide to Periodicals,* which is the reference book for journal and magazine articles generated on certain topics. The researchers borrowed this idea from Bawcom (1995), who also designed an advanced speaking course, and the student questionnaire related to the content was also adapted from hers. The researchers went through the entire the topic index of this guidebook by asking questions such as "Can we provide the material for this?" and "Will it be interesting and enjoyable for our target students?" Based on the above two questions, the researchers ended up with a total of 15 topics. Students were asked to rate these topics with regard to their degree of interests on a four-point scale. Moreover, they were also asked to choose five favorite topics from the list and then rank them in terms of their order of preference with (1) being their first choice and (5) their last one.

On the second section of the student questionnaire, students were provided with a preliminary list of 18 speaking skills that were already elicited from the interviews with the English language instructors and from the writing activity. The students were then asked to rate on both the importance and competence/difficulty they attached to these skills using again a four-point scale on the paper list of objectives.

3.2.1.5 Meeting

A meeting was held to bring the audience group, resource group and also the needs analysts (i.e. researchers) together. The main aim of this meeting was to discuss the tentative goals and objectives of the course to be designed as a result of the information gathered until that time. In other words, the meeting was performed to discuss if these goals and objectives were applicable, realistic and suitable prior to the formulation of the real goals and objectives for the course.

3.2.2 Data analysis procedures

Qualitative and quantitative analyses of the data gathered were conducted to yield data to be used. To make the necessary quantitative data run Predictive Analytics Software Statistics (Version 18) was used. As for the qualitative analysis, a thematic analysis of the interview results was performed.

3.2.3 Results of the needs assessment

3.2.3.1 Results of the writing activity

Results of the analyses on the students' writings were handled under two categories, a) student difficulties/problems/shortcomings and b) student goals. For the difficulties, problems and shortcomings asked through the first question of the writing activity, students reported difficulties with taking part in conversations, pronunciation problems, lack of sufficient practice with speaking skills, lack of activities and entertainment (e.g. films, videos, game-like activities), excessive focus on grammar and also difficulties with reacting to an idea. In relation to the specification of their goals in a further speaking skills course, they mentioned such aims as building speaking confidence, speaking fluently, speaking with a good pronunciation, learning new vocabulary, watching and understanding films, talking before an audience with confidence, having a level in English that will benefit to them at their professional lives and being able to understand a real-life listening text, video film, magazine or newspaper.

3.2.3.2 Results of the teacher interviews

3.2.3.2.1 Results of the interviews with content department teachers

Results of the interviews conducted with three contents teachers (two associate professors and a professor) revealed that students experienced the most difficulty in their content classes with the speaking skills and these difficulties ranged from basic question-answer patterns to extended conversation on a subject in class or on an experiment they did in the laboratories. Another finding related to the confidence level of the students. One academician reported that he felt that the students had a certain level of proficiency in grammatical knowledge, but in class they could not put it into use for communicative purposes and he also observed it with the exam papers written by the students. Though two of the experts mentioned the need for students to talk before the audience as they had student presentations for some topics and they further asserted that the students would need to talk before an audience somewhere in their professional career, one teacher reported that he did not expect students to do a presentation but the students should react to an idea he suggested or should give an answer to and reflect on what he said. All of the academicians agreed on the point that a relatively lower degree of emphasis may be paid to the writing skills in comparison to speaking skills of the students in that students could already manage with the exam papers by using basic mathematics formulas in English. As the teachers were not expecting that much narrative or expository writing from the students as a sort of course requirement, their main concerns were related to the speaking skills. One of the teachers reported that there were some students in their classes who could not even initiate conversations. They suggested that students might like daily topics (like sports, media, technology etc.); however, they should be presented in such a way that will integrate scientific and daily-like information. He provided an example related to this issue by saying:

> "For example, students are very much into Iphones and social networking tools like Facebook and Twitter in their daily lives. Why do not we find a scientific fact about these tools and then connect a factual piece of information from their course content with something more real and congruent with their real lives, which in turn will be more interesting to the students?"

3.2.3.2.2 Results of the interviews with the English language teachers

All three instructors of English recommended that an integrated-skills approach should be followed while teaching speaking. That is, these instructors found it awkward to ask students to speak about something they perhaps have had no earlier knowledge about. One of the teachers explained this idea as follows:

> "Teachers should find and use topics which are familiar to their learners. When there is a completely new piece of information for the students, they should activate learners' pre-knowledge to understand this new piece of information. They should find a way to connect the new piece of information presented to the students with their already existing pre-knowledge in their minds.

They reported that if we attempted to integrate skills as they were already in the real-life, students would feel more confident and learn better. All of the three teachers pointed out the need for the variety of the tasks in the course implementation so as to make the course more interesting to and motivating for the students. The need for a variety of assessment procedures and formative assessment (during the course) was firmly put forth by the teachers based on their assumptions that speaking was a skill always in a continous development and speaking skills need to be monitored in different ways, which in turn makes the lesson varied and interesting for the students. The teachers talked about the incorporation of presentation skills in the course based on the assumption that it might also contribute to students' other courses and later professional lives.

Two of the instructors who were working at a state university where the medium of instruction is English compared their own case to the case here in this current study (i.e. to a university with a 30 % of obligatory English medium of instruction) and recommended that presentation skills should not necessarily include that much strict guidelines and research skills as they have at their university. Alternatively, they suggested us to organize more flexible, less-demanding and real-life relevant mini-presentations for the purposes of the course to be designed. These two instructors mentioned that they benefited a lot from the reaction/reflection type of tasks in which students reflected on their peers' oral speeches through speaking or writing. All three teachers agreed on the idea of offering functional language and phrases (e.g. phrases to start conversation, phrases of agreeing and disagreeing) for the students to use in their conversations. Flexibility especially with regard to the topics for discussion and presentation was another key idea shared and reported by all of the teachers. In also talking about the sub-skill of pronunciation, all three teachers considered it important; but, as a teaching method, they only recommended the teacher presentations of the common problem sounds in class because of time constraints for the speaking course. They also recommended that teachers deal only with the major and very serious pronunciation problems through individual feedback to the students.

3.2.3.2.3   Results of the interviews with students

The analyses of the interview results of the students were handled under two main categories, expectations and problems faced. In talking first about the students' expectations, five out of the six students interviewed in this study pointed out a need to talk before an audience. They considered it important especially for their later professional career and this was consistent with what the English language instructors also suggested. Students complained about their lackings in listening especially when the context was totally unfamiliar to them. Hence, it was seen that they would expect a speaking course that also incorporated listening, which was also consistent with the English language instructors' integrated skills suggestion. It also appears that students like variety in terms of in-class activities and one student contributed to this view by saying as follows:

> "We always have some pair work and then we speak it with the whole class but this is really boring. We need something new. We do not like doing the same activities repeatedly in the class."

Another language skill that the students mentioned that they needed further practice with was identified as vocabulary. The students were found to be eager to learn new vocabulary items. They also complained that given their earlier experiences with English, especially at the preparatory classes, the time devoted to speaking English was limited. Some even complained by saying as in the following:

> "Why are the teachers teaching that much grammar? We need practice of skills but not the practice of such terminology as present simple or present perfect. We need to have more speaking actitivities in order to speak more and better."

In this context, they asserted their major need as more practice in speaking English. Students further asserted that teachers should individuallly deal with them and talk about or inform them about their progress. It was also interesting to see that all of the interviewees expected the teacher to force them to speak by further emphasizing that when they were not directed or controlled by an outside authority, they did not opt to and are not motivated to speak.

Given the problems they encountered in their English language learning practice, students' responses were consistent with their expectations, as it appeared that they expected to improve the areas they felt they had some difficulty in. They mentioned their problems with pronunciation, although they did not attach great importance to this skill. Some students reported that they felt bad with and anxious about their pronunciation. However, the most difficult or problem skill students reported in learning English were found to be speaking and lexical knowledge (vocabulary).

3.2.3.3 Results of the student questionnaire

3.2.3.3.1 Results for the perceived difficulty on the skills

Given the perceived difficulty on the language skills as reported by the study participants, it was seen that all of the students rated the skill, building speaking confidence with varying degrees of difficulty, and nobody rated no difficulty option for this skill, which indeed implies a need for the practice of this skill. Table 1 below depicts the results of the questionnaire on the skills items.

The skill, choosing appropriate presentation topics, has been rated with varying degrees of difficulty by 55.5% of the students, while the remaining 45.5 % expressed that they experienced no difficulty with this skill. The expressed difficulty with this skill is not considerably high, thus demonstrating a moderate to low need for this skill to be practiced by the students. Almost 82% of the students expressed their difficulty for the skill, adjusting language to spoken discourse, and this leads us to conclude that there is a serious need to cover this skill in the advanced speaking course to be designed. Almost 64% of the students rated their perceived difficulty with the skill of using appropriate transitions and signposts by feeling either a certain degree of difficulty or too much difficulty.

Table 1: Perceived Difficulty on the Speaking Skills

	No difficulty (%)	Some difficulty (%)	Difficulty (%)	Too much difficulty (%)
Building speaking confidence*	-	45.5	45.5	9.1
Choosing appropriate presentation topics*	45.5	27.3	9.1	18.2
Adjusting language to spoken discourse*	18.2	36.4	36.4	9.1
Using appropriate transitions and signposts*	36.4	-	54.5	9.1
Expressing and supporting opinions	9.1	45.5	36.4	9.1
Delivering a speech/ presentation*	45.5	27.3	18.2	9.1
Presenting information in an organized way*	36.4	36.4	18.2	9.1
Asking and answering questions*	9.1	72.7	-	9.1
Presenting as a team*	54.5	36.4	-	9.1
Giving and taking the floor*	54.5	18.2	18.3	9.1
Using basic conversational strategies in dialogues	72.7	27.3	-	-
Giving an oral reconstruction*	-	27.3	63.6	9.1
Giving an oral response*	9.1	45.5	27.3	18.2
Reacting to an idea*	-	63.6	27.3	9.1
Reflecting on an idea*	-	36.4	54.5	9.1
Taking part in discussions and debates on various topics*	9.1	27.3	63.6	-
Using correct pronunciation of common problem sounds*	-	60	20	20
Practicing stress and intonation patterns*	9.1	36.4	45.5	9.1

Note. * These objectives were taken/adapted from the course documents on http://mld.metu.edu.tr/tr/node/49

Only 9% of the students reported they perceived no difficulty with the skill, expressing and supporting opinions and this result shows a need to work on this skill in the course to be designed. However, considering the accumulation of preferences on somewhat difficulty degree (i.e. 73% of the participants expressed some difficulty), one can assign a moderate degree of need for this skill in this course. Almost 46% of the respondents reported perceiving no difficulty with delivering a speech or a presentation. In looking at the comparably lower percentages of respondents on the certain degree of or too much difficulty (27%), it is wise to assign a lower degree of need for this skill to meet in the course. Presenting information in an organized way has been rated with varying degrees of difficulty by almost 64% of the students; however, lower percentages were observed concerning a certain degree of difficulty or too much difficulty responses. This leads us to assign a moderate degree of need to practice this strategy in the course. For the skill, asking and answering questions with no difficulty perceptions, 9% of the students rated it with no difficulty responses and 72% of the students rated somewhat difficulty with this item. This result in turn shows that this skill should receive a moderate level of need to be practiced by the learners of the course. Only 9% of the students rated too much difficulty with the item, presenting as a team, and the remaining respondents chose either somewhat difficulty or no difficulty. Therefore, the item received low rating compared to the other skills to be practiced in this course, and it may be even considered for non-inclusion. Following a somewhat similar pattern with the previous skill, the skill of giving and taking the floor appears to be receiving a lower degree of need level among the course objectives as nearly 55% of the students rated no difficulty with this skill. For the skill, using basic conversational strategies in dialogues, almost 73 % of the students responded no difficulty, which in turn addresses a lower emphasis on the course work. The responses for the strategy of giving an oral reconstruction pointed out a need for practice for this strategy in the course as most students perceived varying degrees of difficulties with this skill item. Only 9% of the respondents chose no difficulty for the skill of giving an oral response; however, the emphasis on some difficulty (45.5%) should result in a moderate degree of attention for this skill in the course work. The skill, reacting to an idea follows a somewhat similar pattern to the above skill in that though there are no responses of no difficulty, almost 64% of the students assigned somewhat difficulty for this skill, which again signals a moderate degree of emphasis for this skill in the course. Reflecting on an idea shows an opposite pattern to the above two speaking skills in that the responses for a certain degree of difficulty (54.5%) and too much difficulty (9.1%) were relatively higher than somewhat difficulty degree (36.4%), which again means some degree of attention on this skill within the course design. Students perceived a certain degree of difficulty (63.6%) with the skill, taking part in discussions and debates, which again points out some attention and focus within the class work for this course. Given the remaining two items regarding pronunciation skills, it seems that students reported more difficulty with the stress and intonation patterns (54.6% of students reported difficulty and too much difficulty and 36.4% for some difficulty) in comparison to common problem sounds (40% reported difficulty and too much difficulty and 60% for some difficulty).

    Overall, it seemed that students expressed negatively for the presentation skills (Items 2, 6 and 9). Though the skill, presentating information in an organized way points out a need for the practice of this skill, it seems marginal in that students' perceived difficulty on this skill is more towards the non-difficulty point. Apart from the skill, using basic conversational strategies, other skills appear to deserve consideration and attention in the course work and development.

3.2.3.3.2   Results for the perceived importance on the skills

In looking at the students' responses regarding the importance of the speaking strategies, all strategies were rated important in to varying degrees (see Table 2). The strategy of building speaking confidence received the highest rating of importance with almost 65 % of the students agreed on its importance, while the strategy, choosing appropriate presentation topics received the lowest rating of importance (rated by 9 % of the students as unimportant).

The distribution of the responses for the items 4, 5, 8 and 18 are the same and the responses showed that students confirmed the importance of these items. For the majority of the skills items (Items 1, 2, 3, 4, 5, 6, 8, 10, 11, 12, 13, 14, 15, 16, 17 and 18), it is evident that students attach great importance to the learning and practicing of these skills. For all of the items above, though the distribution of responses differs to some extent, in looking from a general perspective, *important* responses and *very important* responses are relatively more when compared to *somewhat important* and not *important* responses. Moreover, there are only two skills (items 2 and 17) that have received *not important* ratings, but it appears that the frequencies for the unimportant responses are very low and marginal, which again points out an attention over these skills in the course design. Overall, the students considered the skills that the researchers already planned to incorporate in the course based on the review of literature and the interviews with the teachers mentioned earlier in this book. Given the skills, presenting information in an organized way (Item 7) and presenting as a team (Item 9), it appears that the students considered them important, but the degree of importance attached to these items was not strong because the percentage of students responding as somewhat important was higher compared to the percentages from the important and very important degrees. This result is also in line with the degree of difficulty they attached for these items. For another item that received low ratings with regard to the degree of difficulty, that is, the item pertaining to the use of basic conversational strategies, students considered it important, but somewhat important responses were still high.

Overall, all of the speaking strategies surveyed were confirmed for their importance by the students. In talking about the skills relevant to presentation in specific, it is wise to conclude that students confirmed their importance though they had some concerns about the difficulty level they attached to these skills.

Table 2: Perceived Importance of the Speaking Skills

	Not important (%)	Somewhat important (%)	Important (%)	Very important (%)
Building speaking confidence (#1)	-	-	36.4	63.6
Choosing appropriate presentation topics (#2)	9.1	18.2	63.6	9.1
Adjusting language to spoken discourse (#3)	-	18.2	27.3	54.5
Using appropriate transitions and signposts (#4)	-	18.2	54.5	27.3
Expressing and supporting opinions (#5)	-	18.2	54.5	27.3
Delivering a speech/presentation (#6)	-	27.3	45.5	27.3
Presenting information in an organized way (#7)	-	54.5	45.5	-
Asking and answering questions (#8)	-	18.2	54.5	27.3
Presenting as a team (#9)	-	54.5	45.5	-
Giving and taking the floor (#10)	-	36.4	45.5	18.2
Using basic conversational strategies in dialogues (#11)	-	45.5	9.1	45.5
Giving an oral reconstruction (#12)	-	27.3	45.5	27.3
Giving an oral response (#13)*	-	-	18.2	81.8
Reacting to an idea (#14)*	-	-	72.7	27.3
Reflecting on an idea (#15)*	-	18.2	36.4	45.5
Taking part in discussions and debates on various topics (#16)*	-	36.4	36.4	27.3
Using correct pronunciation of common problem sounds (#17)	9.1	9.1	45.5	36.4
Practicing stress and intonation patterns (#18)	-	18.2	54.5	27.3

Note. * These objectives were taken/adapted from the course documents on http://mld.metu.edu.tr/tr/node/49

3.2.3.3.3 Results for the topic selection

Given the student rankings of very interesting responses on the 15 topics included in the student questionnaire, as shown in Table 3, the topic of transportation and travel was rated as very interesting by almost 73 % of the students and this ranking was followed respectively by the topics of health-fitness-beauty and art, human relations, entertainment and media and lastly by education and Turkey. Given the aggregated percentages of responses of very interesting and interesting, no ratings of boring were assigned to the three topics, art, human relations and transportation and travel by the students. Following these three, almost 91 % of the students responded with interest to the topics of health-fitness-beauty, education and Turkey. Likewise, almost 82 % of the students liked the topics of ecology and entertainment-media.

Table 3: Distribution of the Degree of Interests on the Speaking Topics

Topics	Interesting (%)	Very interesting (%)	Interesting/ very interesting (%)
Crime	45.5	18.2	63.6
Education	45.5	45.5	90.9
Ecology	54.5	27.3	81.8
Ethics	20	20	40
Etnicity & stereotyping	36.4	-	36.4
Health & fitness & beauty	27.3	63.6	90.9
Art	36.4	63.6	100
Human relations	45.5	54.5	100
Marketing&money	18.2	45.5	63.6
Personality	36.4	36.4	72.7
Aging	27.3	9.1	36.4
Science & technology	27.3	36.4	63.6
Entertaintment & media	40	50	81.8
Transportation & travel	27.3	72.7	100
Turkey	45.5	45.5	90.9

In order to determine the respondents' rankings of the top five topics, coefficients were assigned in terms of the ranks. Table 4 below shows the results following the assignment of coefficients and our performing necessary calculations. In assigning coefficients (e.g. 5 for 1st rank and 4,3,2,1 etc. for the next ranks respectively) for the topics according to the rank they belong to and then comparing them, five most favorite topics were indicated, in order of interest (by looking cumulatively at the scores of all five ranks) as transportation and travel, human relations, art/Turkey/marketing-money, science and technology/education/ecology (see Table 4).

Table 4: Ranking of Top Five Speaking Topics

Topics	1st rank	2nd rank	3rd rank	4th rank	5th rank
Crime	-	9.1	-	-	9.1
Education	-	-	18.2	9.1	9.1
Ecology	18.2	9.1	-	-	9.1
Ethics	-	-	-	-	-
Etnicity & stereotyping	-	-	-	-	-
Health & fitness & beauty	9.1	-	9.1	9.1	-
Art	18.2	18.2	9.1	-	-
Human relations	-	18.2	27.3	9.1	9.1
Marketing&money	-	9.1	18.2	9.1	9.1
Personality	-	9.1	9.1	-	9.1
Aging	-	-	-	9.1	-
Science&technology	9.1	9.1	-	18.2	-
Entertaintment & media	-	9.1	-	9.1	9.1
Transportation & travel	27.3	-	9.1	18.2	27.3
Turkey	18.2	9.1	-	9.1	9.1

3.3 Reflections from the Needs Assessment to Use in the Design of the Further Speaking Skills Curriculum

Given the results from the teacher and student interviews, student questionnaires and writing activity, valuable insights were gained for several components of the curriculum to be designed. The following presents the major insights derived from the needs assessment in relation to the following stages of the course design (i.e. objectives, content, method, materials and evaluation):

a) Though the speaking will be the main focus of this course, it should be presented in an integrated-skills manner. Therefore, there is a need to specify some objectives for the other language skills, that is, reading, listening and writing. For the speaking skills, objectives should encompass the basic and main skills of speaking (e.g. asking and answering questions and reacting to an idea).

b) There is a need to identify objectives pertaining to the presentation skills; however, these objectives should include non-strict presentation requirements and be connected to everyday, real life-like activities. Student questionnaire results concerning the difficulty level for the skills provided in the questionnaire forms were not consistent with the information gained from the student interviews, teacher interviews and writing activity especially with regard to the incorporation of presentation skills or ability to speak before an audience. However, the importance of presentation skills was emphasized by the teachers (both English and content teachers) based on the assumption that these skills would be useful for the students for their future professional lives and other courses.

c) There is a need to incorporate objectives to help students enhance their speaking confidence (i.e. affective goals and objectives) and organize instructional practices accordingly.

d) Conversation strategies should be included in the course work. The term basic conversational strategies in the student questionnaires may have mislead the students in the sense that they may not need to work on basic conversational strategies again since they have already taken the basic level strategies at the preperatory classes. However, as their proficiency levels proceed, they may need some other strategies and some other ways of using functional language. As is also supported with the interview data from the English language instructors, there is a need to offer functional language/phrases (e.g. phrases to start and end conversations, phrases of agreeing and disagreeing) so that the students can use these phrases in their future conversations and presentations.

e) There should be objectives mainly related to the development of reading skills (and also listening) and expanding vocabulary for there is a need to form contexts for the students to elaborate on ideas for their speaking purposes. Students should be exposed to new concepts and learn new information, which may necessiate a focus on the receptive skills of the language through which the students will receive the necessary input. In this regard, reading skills of the students should be developed for the sake of their gaining better speaking skills.

f) There is a need to specify objectives and activities for pronunciation skills. Though the need for improving pronunciation ability has been emphasized by the students and the teachers, there should be a moderate degree of focus by helping the students with common problems of pronunciation (common problem sounds for Turks and some stress patterns etc.) or when a specific need arises in the course time.

g) There is a need to organize a variety of activities that will motivate the students.

h) There should be flexibility in the choice of topics, and when talking about a topic, in the light of this flexibility, students should be given chances to handle it from different viewpoints. Using the needs assessment results for topic selection, 10 out of 15 topics were selected to include in the speaking course curricula. Though some of these topics have been rated more than the others, the researchers decided to leave the choice to the teachers when putting this curriculum into practice depending on the characteristics of their students. Therefore, a bulk of topics were provided for teachers to choose. For instance, the topic of science and technology was included depending on the suggestions received from the interviews with

the teachers though this topic was not very popular in the questionnaires responded by the students. The writers of this book mainly recommend the topics of art, human relations, transportation and travel, science and technology and health-fitness and beauty to be used as a course content in this course.
i) Topics chosen should offer recent and up-to-date information that makes the class more interesting to the students.
j) A variety of assessment procedures is required, and formative assessment should be a part of the course assessment plan.
k) There is a need to incorporate real-life practices and applications for the classroom tasks in the lessons. Some students set goals related to their being able to understand real life materials such as videos, newspapers or films. In this context, students should be exposed to real-life material and input from the real life.

Based on the above insights, the researchers compiled the course goals and objectives and discussed this list in the meeting that is the last instrument of the needs assessment plan mentioned earlier in this chapter. One of the English language instructors interviewed, a group of interviewed students and the researchers came together to discuss this list of tentative goals and objectives. The researchers basically outlined the tentative list of objectives to the audience in the meeting that took place in a social gathering manner at the school's cafeteria, and asked their last words and reactions concerning the course goals and objectives in order to polish and improve the tentative list of objectives. The well-defined list of objectives was still tentative in this stage because the researchers wanted to check them with the relevant literature prior to presenting the final form of objectives for the course.

4. Curriculum Design

4.1 Description and Components of the Curriculum Design Model Used

Graves' (2000) language course design model and Posner and Rudnitsky's (1997) course design model were both utilized in the design of this course (see Appendix G and Appendix H for Graves' and Posner and Rudnitsky's course design models respectively). In other words, a new course design model for this course design work was adapted from these two popular frameworks above. The following account provides the necessary information and the details about this new curriculum design model specifically adapted from the above two models (see Appendices H and I for the two course design models).

The course design model used in the design of the further speaking course (FSC) includes the main characteristics and elements of curriculum development as expected; however, this new course design model possesses a non-linear form and flow (though the shape depicts a linear one) and it particularly emphasizes the processes rather than the products during the course design process, which thus makes it possible for us to consider it different from most known course design models in the literature (see Figure 1). One can easily recognize the processes described as *verbs* in the course design model adapted for the purposes of this study and it is appearent that each process in the model ends with a product.

It is important to know that there are two fundamental characteristics of the model. The first one refers to the absence of hierarchy and sequence among the processes included in the model. Course designers are able to start the course design work at any point they find it appropriate and logical. Such decisions as to where to start the course design are in fact related to the course designers' own belifs and opinions and also to the course rationale. Therefore, the two processes in the model, *articulating beliefs* and *defining context* have been placed at the bottom of the graphical representation of the model so as to emphasize that these two processes will act as backbones and foundational processes to form and guide all of the other subsequent processes in the model. The second characteristic is related to the functioning of a systems approach to course design. Such an approach is portrayed in the model to emphasize that all the processes and products are interrelated. If these processes and products are interrelated, it will be also true that each of these processes and products influence and is also influenced by the other processes and products in the model.

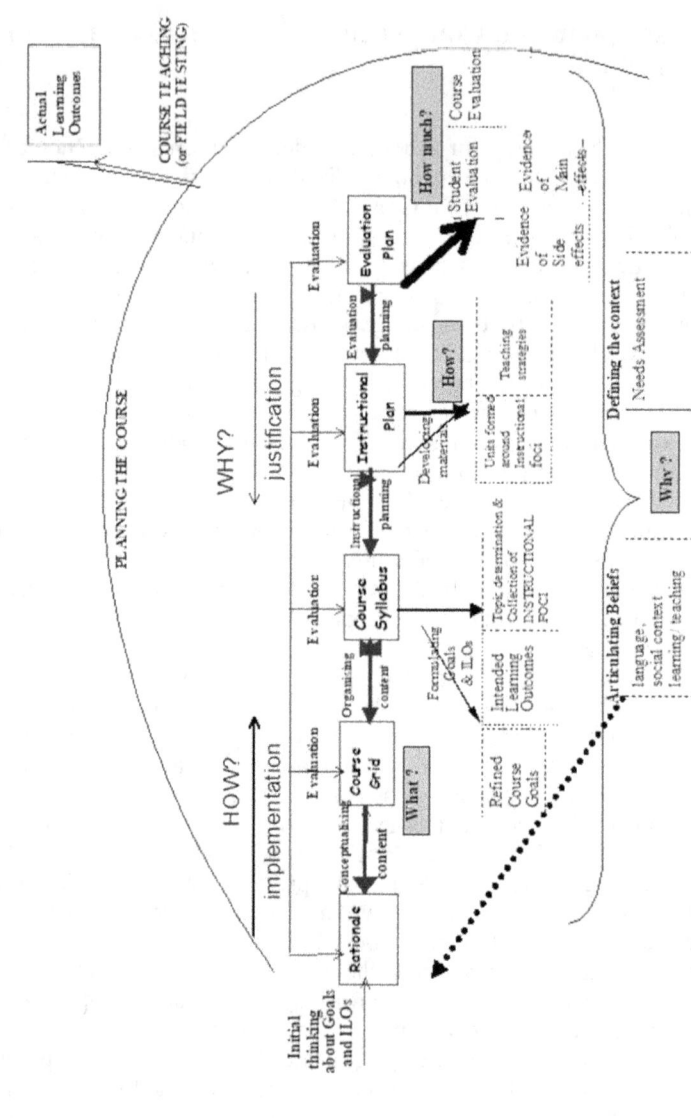

Figure 1. Course Design Model for The Further Speaking Skills Course

For this reason, course designers are to consider all of the components included in the model at the same time. However, it is also possible that course designers can change between components before exactly completing one component, which shows that the model has no designated route of flow and procedural steps. The researchers tried to emphasize this with the use of two-way arrows in the graphical representation of the model. In this sense, you may return to the previous steps you have already covered because you perhaps become more equipped with new opinions and ideas as you proceed with the other components. Likewise, it is possible to think about the course content and some possible instructional events even before you derive your rationale for the course. The model offers no step-by-step guide to course design. Although the model figure (shape) may contribute to this outlook by its form (the researchers oversimplified the process here), it should be interpreted as a non-linear one.

The proposed course design model is mainly composed of two main components called *processes* and *products*. There are seven processes involved in the model: a) conceptualizing content, b) organizing content, c) instructional planning, d) formulating goals and intended learning outcomes (ILOs), e) developing materials, f) intitial thinking about the goals and ILOs and g) evaluation planning. The preliminary five processes were adopted from Graves (2000) and the last two processes were taken from the course design model developed by Posner and Rudnitsky's (1997). The relevant products based upon the above processes are course grid (map) and course syllabus which were taken from Graves' (2000) course design framework. The products also included instructional plan and evaluation plan that were taken from Posner and Rudnitsky's (1997) instructional design framework.

There are two foundational steps in the course design process. These are *articulating beliefs and defining context* and these stages refer to a detailed understanding of the students, physical context and resources. *Articulating beliefs* is related to the course designers' opinions concerning the language, social context and learning and teaching process. The process of *articulating beliefs* as Graves (2000) summarized in terms of the three main elements, language, social context and learning/teaching is seen very important because our opinions come before our decisions and actions. That is, it is our opinions and beliefs that guide our actions and decisions to do something and here to design and teach a course.

Defining context, another process in course design, helps the course designers to understand the resources and challenges to understand the real context of the course to be designed, which will be later used in forming their decisions regarding the course rationale. Defining context also encompasses *needs assessment* in which course designers gather information concerning the current situation of the learners (i.e. their level of proficiencies, attitudes towards the language, likes and dislikes) and the future situation of the learners (i.e. their expectations from this course, their language skills and structures aimed to be developed by the end of this course). Accordingly, defining context has been located at the very bottom part of the model as it represents a foundation or a starting point for the other components in the course design model.

There are two main processes, *conceptualizing content and organizing content* related to content specification in this course design model. *Conceptualizing content* can be described as a process during which course designers or teachers identify and determine the most crucial content for their students based upon their inferences regarding the main goals of the course to be designed and students' needs and expectations from this course. It is within this process of conceptualizing content where the course designers choose what to include, emphasize or exclude in relation to their course content. According to Graves (2000), this process ends with a product generated in the format of a mind-map, a flowchart or a grid, which may be a sort of draft syllabus for the course to be developed. By exactly following Graves' (2000) principles, the researchers recommend the conceptualizing of content according to three main categories, a) language, b) social context and c) learning and the learner. Accordingly, it is this categorization that helps the course designers have a first version of the course content. *Organizing content* can be described as a process during which the course designers further the process of conceptualizing content in that they now make more informed decisions about the content and specifically about the organizing principles that will compose and integrate the content. Hence, the course developers or teachers have a firmly established and fully-developed form of the course content with the help of this process. The end product as a result of organizing content will be a full and finalized form of the course schedule or a course grit.

Formulating goals and objectives (intended learning outcomes) is a process through which course designers firmly establish the direction and rationale of the course to be designed. The rationale of the course to be designed is formulated by the articulation of beliefs about social context and learning/teaching and and also by the definition of the context as a result of needs evaluation.

Planning instruction encompasses planning decisions regarding teaching techniques and activities to be performed in the course and regarding the specification of the unit content. Teaching techniques and activities is presented together with the determination of unit content (i.e. forming units around instructional focus; see Posner & Rudnitsky, 1997) based on the frequent assumption that instructional activities and materials have an influence on the specification of the unit content in language courses.

Given the *planning evaluation* component of FSC model, course designers make plans regarding evaluation and they are expected to come up with the two evaluation products, a) evaluation plan for student's learning and b) evaluation plan for the course.

As is also offered by Graves (2000), course design, as shown in Figure 2, involves four fundamental stages, a) planning for the course to be designed, b) teaching the course, c) evaluating the course and planning it again based on the evaluation data and finally d) teaching the course again based on the second round of planning decisions.

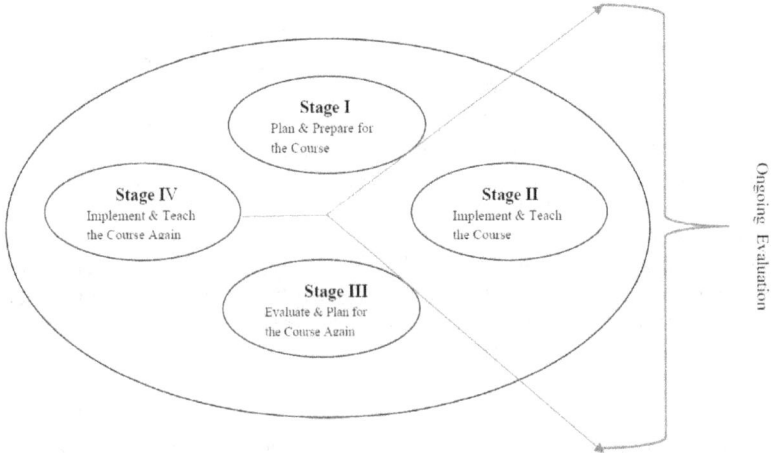

Figure 2. The Cycle of Course Development (adapted from Graves, 2000, p. 10)

The FSC model devised mainly centers on Stage I that refers to planning a new course. That is, no implementation takes place on the model because it in fact takes place at the second main stage of the model, teaching the course. The course syllabus indicates what is to be learnt, course rationale indicates why is to be learnt, the instructional plan informs how to enhance learning and lastly assessment plan explains how to evaluate student learning and effectiveness of the course. However, none of these planning processes result in any learning due to no actual implementation. However, for the purposes of FSC model adapted, the researchers added this teaching or field testing process (placed outside the semi-cycle-like shape on the FSC model's graphical representation) so as to show that only after some implementation (teaching/field testing), that is, only after the actual instruction process and accompanied learner engagement, one can see the results, that is, whether something is learned or not and whether intended learning outcomes are turned into actual learning outcomes.

4.2 Application of the Model to the Further Speaking Course

4.2.1 *Articulating beliefs*

We condiser the component of articulating beliefs to be important in a course design project as every further step in the course design will be directly linked to one's beliefs as a language teacher or a course designer, where you as an educational expert are coming from, what inspires and guides you in the choices you will make in the course design process. Stern (1992) claims that information about *language, society, learning* and *teaching* should be sufficiently sought in order to form a theory for teaching languages. Therefore, it is wise to begin with talking about each of these concepts along with one's beliefs as a language teacher (or a course designer) before one really develops his or her own theory of teaching for the FSC. Thus, the following presents articulation of one of the researchers, Dr. Gülçin Mutlu's, an English teacher's beliefs guiding the design of the FSC.

> In terms of *my view of language*, I believe that language is an exchange of information and a way of communicative interaction. This idea has always been a driving force behind my teaching. This belief is based on or shaped by my experience as a learner at university. The school where I was a student did not follow a communicatively-oriented curriculum. In our course for speaking, we followed a fixed textbook including discussion questions assigned for each lesson. We memorized and rehearsed before we spoke in class. The teacher corrected each and every grammatical mistake in our speech utterances. That was all in this course. There was no interaction, negotiation or participation. In other words, we were just telling about a story by heart, not in fact talking to someone or communicating in our speaking course. Trembling with fear of making mistakes, we waited for our turns to speak. In the following years of my four-year training period at university, I realized that my friends and I were not able to participate in oral conversations easily. In the real world, language exchange was not a type of discussion question we could memorize earlier. Yes, I was competent in the speaking course according to the assessment of my teacher; however, I still did not know how to use language for my communicative purposes. This kind of linguistic competency should not be the norm for my own students. All of my experiences as a learner formed the basis of my own beliefs and principles for my own teaching. They prompted me to exploit some guiding principles that I would not prefer my students experience the same things I had encountered in my own learning situation. If I want my students to be proficient in a language, then they should be com-

municatively competent as language is for communication. This idea shapes all my teaching, not only in terms of speaking skills. I also view language as a meaningful whole. Therefore, my teaching emphasizes the interpretation and comprehension of overall meaning, not each and every detail in a given language sample (e.g., a poem, a reading passage or a short dialogue). For *my view of learners and learning*, I see my students as active participants in class. They should initiate, negotiate and communicate in class. They are the makers of knowledge. In this sense, I view learning as a process of problem solving and discovery by learners. In terms of *my beliefs about teaching and the role of the teacher*, I view my teaching from two different ends. I am the possessor of knowledge, and I transmit it to my students at one end. This requires me to act more authoritatively in that I decide what to teach myself, provide examples and guide my students at every step they take. At the other end, I see teaching is a collaborative process in which I negotiate the knowledge and the decisions with my learners, and we share what we have. I see myself as a life-long learner. I may learn from my students, as well. This role requires me to be much more flexible and less authoritative and to act as a facilitator while it should be my students who take the responsibilities of their own learning. Briefly, in my teaching, I may wear too many hats! (i.e. I may assume various roles as a teacher). In terms of *my view of social context*, I emphasize that my students should possess the pragmatic and practical knowledge in combination with grammatical knowledge. They should know how to adapt their language according to the social context and to the person they are speaking to. I always emphasize this issue by pointing out to the issues of register and formal-informal ways of saying in some parts of my class time.

4.2.2 Defining the context and needs assessment

In defining the context for the FSC, all information relevant to learner analyses of the FSC course (learners characteristics, proficiency levels, learning styles and preferences), learner and their learning needs, and contextual characteristics (resources and challenges) were reported. The learner and contextual characteristics part of the FSC design model have been already discussed respectively in the first (introduction) and third (needs assessment) chapters of this work. You may refer to the first and third chapters to see the application of the model regarding this component.

4.2.3 Formulating goals and rationale

4.2.3.1 Goals

Definition of the context supported by the needs assessment results and also by the articulation of beliefs in relation to language, social context and learning/teaching helped us formulate the goals of the FSC. When formulating the goals of the FSC, we were attentive to the results of the needs assessment and the reflections (see Chapter 3 for the reflections from the needs assessment) based on it. As the course needs to be presented in an integrated-skills manner with a particular emphasis upon speaking skills and with the other skills to be used as a springboard for the development of speaking skills, we formulated a main goal related to speaking skills, another goal including the other remaining skills of language to be used as a springboard and in a recycling format to serve the main goal of developing speaking skills and also one affective goal in line with the need for building confidence in speaking. Such decions about the formulation of goals were taken based upon the results from the needs evaluation elicited from English language teachers and the literature review on teaching speaking skills. Two somehow longer term intended learning outcomes (goals), understanding of oral communication and transfer of what students gained in relation to the practice of speaking skills were also considered among the main goals of this course. As our initial thinking about the goals of this course will be much more elaborated later, the goals will be refined following the organization of the course content.

4.2.3.2 Course rationale

Speaking skills as one of the two productive skills of general language ability take time to develop and speaking develops with practice. It appears that students usually gain other language skills more easily than the spoken language skills. As a reason for this implication, they complain about their difficulty with the spoken language and limited amount of time allocated to this skill especially when compared to the time allocated to reading and grammar and sometimes to listening. Therefore, students usually feel themselves more confident with reading rather than speaking. In this sense, Further Speaking Skills is a course the purpose of which is to begin onwards (following students preperatory year) to help the students to gain the necessary speaking skills to study in accordance with the English language as a medium of instruction policy followed in their main faculty curricula (content departments). Moreover, this course also aims to help the students to cope with the communication demands of daily and professional life that the students are facing or are to face with in the future.

4.2.4 Conceptualizing content and course grid

Our conceptualization of the course content is drawn from various sources, such as the results from the needs assessment and the questions that we pose to ourselves as teachers and course designers. Graves (2000) provides a good list of questions (see Figure 3 below) that may guide us in conceptualizing the content of this course. We also added a fifth question, which is "What do I need to emphasize, cover or drop in my course?" These five main questions also helped us to shape the content of this course, that is, what we will explicitly teach or explicitly emphasize in the FSC. After conceptualizing the content (i.e., knowing what to teach and how to deal with in this course), we may better know where we desire the students to go with this course. In this way, it gets easier for us to formulate the course objectives to arrive at our goals in this FSC.

> 1. What shoud the students learn in this course in terms of their characteristics, their needs* and the aim of the course?
> 2. What are the alternatives concerning what they can learn in this course?
> 3. What are the contributing and hindering factors of the course that may influence and limit our available alternatives concerning the content?
> 4. What are the relationships among the altenatives considered for the determination of course content?

Figure 3: Questions Guiding Conceptualizing Content (adapted from Graves' framework, 2000, p. 38; * The information about the needs may be generated from the needs assessment).

Following these guiding questions, we employed the framework for organizing the categories for conceptualizing content suggested by Graves (2000). We marked (with a √) under each category to depict the sub-categories we initially thought to incorporate in the FSC (see Figure 4).

Focus on Language		
linguistic skills	situations	Reading √ e.g. understanding written texts (input)
topics/themes √ e.g. what the language is used to talk about	Tasks √ e.g. what you can do with the foreign language	Speaking √ e.g. oral skills, producing fluent stretches of discourse
competencies	content	Writing √ e.g. producing written texts
communicative functions	genre	listening √ e.g. aural comprehension skills (input)
Focus on Learning and Learners		
affective objectives √	interpersonal skills √	learning strategies
Focus on Social Context		
sociolinguisitic skills √	sociocultural skills	sociopolitical skills √ e.g. developing skills for making criticism and interpreting the conditions accordingly

Figure 4: Categories to Choose for the Conceptualisation of Content (adapted from Graves' framework, 2000, p. 43 & 53)

Based on our ways of content conceptualization, we generated the following grid (Figure 5), which is somehow the initial representation of the FSC curriculum.

Topic/Theme	Activities	Skills*	Sub-skills By the end of the course, should know	Goals (*Initial Thinking)
• Transportation and travel • Health-fitness-beauty • Art • Human relations • Turkey • Entertainment and media • Science and Tecnology	Reading texts, discussions, performing role plays, pair work, group work.	wr/sp/l/r	• Listening for specific information* • Listening for the main idea* • Reading for the main idea* • Reading for specific information • Scanning • Identifying different opinions • Evaluating different viewpoints • Making connections between ideas • Expanding vocabulary & activating passive vocabulary • Synthesizing • Paraphrasing • Writing a reaction/response paragraphs/short essay • Giving an oral reconstruction • Giving an oral response* • Reacting to an idea* • Reflecting on an idea* • Expressing opinions (agreement and disagreement) • Taking part in discussions and debates on various topics* • Using correct pronunciation of common problem sounds* • Using appropriate transitions and signposts • Delivering a speech/presentation • Building speaking confidence • Adjusting language to spoken discourse	• "Students will be able to utilize the skills of listening and speaking for the purposes of socializing, providing and obtaining information, expressing personal feelings and opinions, persuading others to adopt a course of action in the targeted topic areas." (Graves, 2000, p. 82) • "Students will be able to utilize the skills of reading and writing for the purposes of socializing, providing and obtaining information, expressing personal feelings and opinions, persuading others to adopt a course of action in the targeted topic areas." (Graves, 2000, p. 82) • Students will be able to utilize the skills of making effective presentations required according to the targeted topic areas and in given formats (current events, mini-presentation etc.) by the teacher. • Students will be able to develop positive attitude towards the speaking discourse and activities.

Figure 5: Course Grid for the FSC; Note: * These objectives were taken/adapted from the course documents on http://mld.metu.edu.tr/node/49

4.2.5 Organizing the course and course syllabus.

As suggested by Graves (2000), five overlapping processes were employed for organizing the course content that has been already broadly conceptualized (by using several categories) and put into a grid format above. The following (Figure 6) shows the procedures followed.

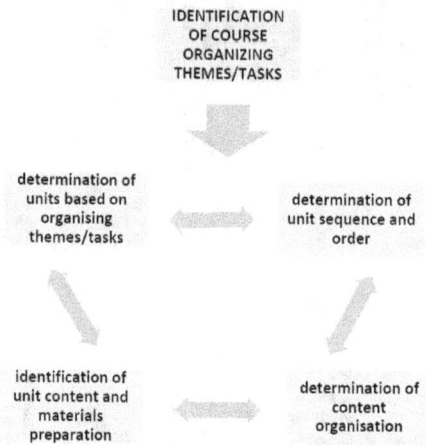

Figure 6: Five Aspects of Organizing a Course (adapted from Graves, 2000, p. 150)

The processes do not follow a specific order. As we have decided, the underlying principle of the FSC course will be the *themes*. That is, the FSC is organized around themes/topics, and each theme/topic will be the focus of each unit. The identification of the course units based on the organizing principles of themes/topics was performed using the data from the needs assessment. The analyses of questionnaire data in relation to topic selection revealed the popularity of following topics of art, transportation and travel, human relations, health-fitness-beauty, entertainment and media.

The topics are not sequenced, as there is no specific progression for the themes chosen in the needs assessment, and it is left to the teacher to determine the sequence of units. Moreover, as the course proceeds, the teacher may make more factual choices in relation to the organization and sequence of the topics. The determination of unit content refers to the determination of language and skills content of the course. In this regard, this course revolves around speaking skills that will be supported by the remaining language skills. In this regard, the content organization based on the review of literature on second language acquisition theoretical framework may follow the principle of content building (Graves, 2000, p.136) specified as "A provides knowledge or skills required to do or understand B (or B builds on knowledge and skills provided by A)". In this regard, our unit organization revolves around a cycle which begins with a language input (either through listening or reading), followed by a focus on speaking and an oral presentation and ends with writing or speaking activity. Therefore, the unit organization follows cyclic nature (Graves, 2000) which refers to the occurrence of a predictable sequence for the content presentation of the FSC. The key to our content organization is the idea of recycling (spiraling). Our preferred way of recycling that stands for "the reintroduction of something learnt in line with something else so that it could be reused and learned in more depth" (Graves, 2000, p. 138) includes recycling a skill using a different skill. Hence, the content of the FSC brings together the skills of listening, reading, speaking and listening, which are presented in a cycle and also uses the topics/themes as unifying foci. The content we determined and organized should be in accordance with the intended learning outcomes determined based on the results from the needs assessment and partly on the review of literature. The following first presents the refined course goals and their alignment with the intended learning outcomes. This alignment is later employed for the generation of course syllabus (see Figure 7 on p. 58 for the course syllabus together with the list of goals and intended learning outcomes).

4.2.6 Refined course goals and intended learning outcomes

We initially thought about the goals on a previous section of this work; but, as it is possible to come back to an earlier step to refine it in line with the non-hierarchical nature of the course design model employed, we find it wiser to come back to our course goals when working on the objectives because objectives would lead to the actualization of our course goals. We have arrived at the following list of related objectives (aligned with the goals) with the help of our own perception and evaluation of the needs assessment mentioned earlier and also of the review of literature conducted.

We used Stern's (1992) framework of *cognitive goals, proficiency goals, affective goals* and *transfer goals* when formulating the course goals. The terminology we used for the course objectives was borrowed from Posner and Rudnitsky's (1997) *intended learning outcomes* (ILOs) because the idea behind the three words, intended, learning and outcome appeared meaningful to us. We only used the terminology Posner and Rudnitsky (1997) came up with and we did not categorize the ILOs into four classes of cognitions, cognitive skills, psycho-motor perceptual skills and affects as he recommended. Instead, we used such components as performance and condition from Mager (1975) framework for most of our ILOs by following a flexible and easy wording.

4.2.6.1 Goals and intended learning outcomes for FSC

Proficiency (High Priority Goals and Intended Learning Outcomes)

Goal 1: By the end of the course, students will be able to develop their speaking skills for the purposes of effective oral communication with others, "socializing, providing and obtaining information, expressing personal feelings and opinions, persuading others to adopt a course of action in the targeted topic areas." (Graves, 2000, p. 82).

ILO 1a: Students will be able to adjust language to spoken discourse when required by the targeted activity within a unit on the targeted topic area.

ILO 1b: Students will be able to use appropriate transitions and signposts when talking and/or discussing about the oral activities organized for a unit on the targeted topic areas.

ILO 1c: Students will be able to express and support opinions when talking and/or discussing about the oral activities organized for a unit on the targeted topic areas.

ILO 1d: Students will be able to ask and answer questions in their conversations, face-to-face, with the teacher and their classmates.

ILO 1e: Students will be able to give an oral reconstruction of the information they gain through reading or listening input using their own novel words and expressions.

ILO 1f: Students will be able to give an oral response to the questions directed by their classmates and teachers.

ILO 1g: Students will be able to react to an idea posed by their friends or teachers or by the reading or listening input provided in the units about the targeted topic areas.

ILO 1h: Students will be able to reflect on an idea posed by their friends or teachers or by the reading or listening input provided in the units about the targeted topic areas.

ILO 1i: Students will be able to take part in discussions and debates on various topics included in the activities of a unit about the targeted topic areas.

ILO 1j: Students will be able to use conversational strategies in their dialogues or discussions (i.e. in their oral communication) provided by the teacher as functional (operational) language patterns.

Goal 2: By the end of the course, students will be able to develop their presentation skills or basically their ability to speak before an audience.

ILO 2a: Students will be able to deliver a presentation on the assigned topic areas and formats (mini presentations, current news event presentation etc.) by the teacher.

ILO 2b: Students will be able to present information in an organized way for in-class activities assigned by the teacher.

ILO 2c: Students will be able to choose appropriate presentation topics for in-class activities assigned and informed by the teacher.

ILO 2d: Students will be able to give and take the floor when presenting as a team or a group for an in-class activity assigned by the teacher.

Goal 3 By the end of the course, students will be able to develop their pronunciation skills that they appear to be experiencing problems.

ILO 2a: Students will be able to use correct pronunciation of common problem sounds and also those sounds identified by research as the problems sounds for Turkish learners (e.g. –th sound, past tense –ed pronunciation, pronunciation of silent letters, schwa pronunciation)

ILO 2b: Students will be able to produce appropriate stress (word level stress, sentence level stress) and intonation patterns in English (e.g. rising intonation and falling intonation with yes/no or –wh questions)

Cognitive

Goal 3: By the end of the course, students will articulate the elements of and what constitutes 'good speaking and communication'.

ILO 3a: Students will be able to demonstrate knowledge of functional/operational language to use for their oral communication purposes.

ILO 3b: Students will demonstrate knowledge of basic pronunciation that will help them to pronounce words, phrases and sentences intelligibly.

ILO 3c: Students will demonstrate knowledge of how to start, follow, give examples and end their oral conversations (in debates, discussions, dialogues and presentations etc.)

Transfer

Goal 4: By the end of the course, students will have developed strategies to transfer what they have gained with the practice of one skill into some other skill format (from speaking to writing, from reading to speaking, from listening to speaking etc.

ILO 4a: Students will be able to gain an understanding of an input (reading or listening) later to be used for speaking using several skills and strategies they have already gained in their earlier experience with English[1]

ILO 4b: Students will be able to transfer what they have gained through the input-speaking-output cycle into a writing output for in-class activities[2] assigned and informed by the teacher.

Goal 5: By the end of the course, students will have developed strategies to improve their speaking abilities.

ILO 5a: Students will be able to articulate how to use functional operational language that promotes speaking.

ILO 5b: Students will develop a set of speaking abilities, such as reacting to an idea, reflecting on an idea, making an oral reconstruction to cope with various oral communication tasks.

ILO 5c: Students will be able to brainstorm and articulate ideas regarding the strategies to promote speaking skills

ILO 5d: Students will be able to articulate how they can practice and apply particular areas of knowledge and experience that they have gained in the FSC in their other courses.

ILO 5e: Students will be able to articulate how they can transfer and use some speaking skills in other areas of their life (i.e., work, school, and personal).

Goal 6: By the end of the course, students will have developed strategies to improve their ability to speak before an audience.

ILO 6a: Students will be able to articulate how to behave in front of an audience

ILO 6b: Students will be able to distinguish a good presentation topic

ILO 6c: Students will be able to know how to present information in an organized way

---

1 Reading for the main idea; Reading for specific information; Making inferences & interpretations; Reading for details; Reading between the lines; Skimming; Scanning; Identifying different opinions; Evaluating different viewpoints; Making connections between ideas; Reading extensively to gather data; Sorting through & prioritizing information; Expanding vocabulary & activating passive vocabulary; Listening between the lines; Listening for specific information; Listening for the main idea; Note taking; * The above skills and strategies for reading and listening were taken from http://mld.metu.edu. tr/tr/node/49)

2 Writing speech analysis reports; Writing self evaluation reports; Synthesizing; Paraphrasing; Summarizing

Affective

Goal 7: By the end of the course, students will develop confidence in their ability to speak in English.

Objectives 7a: Students will be able to document their strengths as speakers, identifying the areas (e.g. pronunciation, conversational ability or the use of functional patterns) in which they are successful.

Objectives 7b: Students will develop an awareness about certain sub-skills of speaking (e.g., pronunciation, talking before an audience, taking part in discussions etc.) and the contributions of practicing them for developing speaking skills.

Objectives 7c: Students will be able to confidently initiate, attend and sustain conversations, face-to-face, with the teacher and the classmates.

HIGH PRIORITY INTENDED LEARNING OUTCOMES (*specified in detail above)	GOALS
Building speaking confidence **Choosing appropriate presentation topics** **Presenting as a team** **Delivering a speech/presentation** **Presenting information in an organized way** Adjusting language to spoken discourse Using appropriate transitions and signposts Expressing and supporting opinions Asking and answering questions Giving and taking the floor Using conversational strategies in dialogues Giving an oral reconstruction Giving an oral response Reflecting on an idea Reacting to an idea Taking part in discussions and debates on various topics **Using correct pronunciation of common problem sounds** **Practicing stress and intonation patterns**	• By the end of the course, students will be able to develop their speaking skills for the purposes of effective oral communications with others, "socializing, providing and obtaining information, expressing personal feelings and opinions, persuading others to adopt a course of action in the targeted topic areas." (Graves, 2000, p. 82). • By the end of the course, students will develop confidence in their ability to speak in English. • By the end of the course, students will have developed strategies to transfer what they have gained with the practice of one skill into some other skill format (from speaking to writing, from reading to speaking, from listening to speaking etc.) • By the end of the course, students will have developed strategies to improve their speaking abilities. (long-term) • By the end of the course, students will be able to develop their presentation skills or basically their ability to speak before an audience. • By the end of the course, students will have developed strategies to improve their ability to speak before an audience. • By the end of the course, students will articulate the elements of an1 what constitutes 'good speaking and communication'. (long-term)

MODERATE PRIORITY INTENDED LEARNING OUTCOMES (*specified in detail above)		GOALS (cont.)
Reading for the main idea	Listening between the lines	**The topics available for Weeks 1-15** Transportation and travel Education Health-fitness-beauty Turkey Art Science and technology Human relations Entertainment and media Marketing-money
Reading for specific information	Listening for specific information	
Making inferences & interpretations	Listening for the main idea	
Reading for details	Note taking	
Reading between the lines	Writing speech analysis reports	
Skimming	Writing self evaluation reports	
Scanning	Synthesizing	
Identifying different opinions	Paraphrasing	
Evaluating different viewpoints		
Making connections between ideas		
Reading extensively to gather data		
Sorting through & prioritizing information		
Expanding vocabulary & activating passive vocabulary		

Suggested activities for going one step further by speaking strand:
Role-plays
Discussions
Debates *see Appendix A for a list of activities)

WEEKS 1-2	WEEKS 4-5	WEEKS 7-8	WEEKS 10-11	WEEKS 13-14
Unit Presentation	Unit Presentation	Unit Presentation	Unit Presentation	Unit Presentation
WEEK 3 Sts presentation	WEEK 6 Sts Presentation	WEEK 9 MIDTERM	WEEK 12 Sts presentation	WEEK 15 Sts presentation & Wrap up

UNIT PRESENTATION
- **Getting started**: Reading and/or Listening activity + setting the stage of a speaking activity
- **Going one step further by speaking**: More speaking activity + setting the stage for the presentation activity
- **Putting it all together**: Speaker Presentation Activity
- **Recycling it in another form**: recycling the skill with other skills (writing, oral discussions etc.)

STUDENT PRESENTATION: *Provide presentation guidelines in line with the topic you have covered

Figure 7. Curriculum for FSC

4.2.7 Instructional planning and an instructional plan for the FSC

In order to come up with an instructional plan, we need to work on the course curriculum we devised in most parts and the instruction we envision to put into practice. Here again we worked in more than one parts of the curriculum design model we adapted by paying attention to the tripartite relationship between the intended learning outcomes, conceptualized and organized content and the instructional practices to be employed. We attempted to plan a series of events around materials, and therefore we leaped back to the organization of content that we had decided as a cycle of skills (moving from input to more output), which stands for the format of within unit sequencing. However, we had not specified the instructional events that will take place within each unit. Hence, our instructional planning included two main procedures, *forming unit content around instructional foci* and *developing teaching strategies* (instructional practices). The idea behind forming units around instructional foci stems from the way we conceptualized and organized the course content. We have topics, we have the ILOs of the FSC, and now it is time to combine them with instructional activities centering on the topics we determined, and we need to develop materials (e.g. reading or listening texts, pictures, videos etc.) to put these instructional techniques into practice. Therefore, the processes of conceptualizing and organizing content and developing materials are all interconnected, which required us to move back and forth on the model many times. When some pieces of potential instructional foci are found, and they are evaluated considering their appropriateness for the ILOs, appropriateness for the learners' abilities, potential for motivation and feasibility.

In talking about the units formed around instructional foci, they are indeed formed around themes (thus each theme becoming an instructional focus). Each theme would serve as a vehicle for learning the course, and each unit is taught through a number of more specific instructional foci, which could be reading or listening texts, videos or films. Hence, the themes and more specifically the materials developed introduce content into the course that is not evident in ILOs but serve as devices for accomplishing ILOs.

4.2.8 Methods (teaching) strategies

With the teaching strategies, we aimed to design the right tasks that will help us use the instructional foci and thus content we devised for the FSC in an effective way. On the way to accomplish this aim, we received the most help from the review of literature on teaching. The following discusses the guidelines for the preparation of activities for the course. Most ideas were taken from

Graves' (2000) synthesis in her book for designing activities for language teaching.

- Activities should refer to students' needs outside the class. There should be real-life relevance. (authenticity)
- Activities should lead students to be engaged in problem-solving, discovery and analyses. (problem solving and discovery)
- Activities should develop the skills that students will use for authentic communication. (authenticity)
- Activities should be authentic as much as possible for authentic activities develop learners' real language use. (authenticity)
- Activities should present opportunities to vary roles and groupings. (role-plays and pair and group work)
- Activities should be presented in various formats. (variety of tasks/activities)
- Activities should employ authentic texts and realia in order for students to access the language as it is put into use in real life. ((authenticity)
- Activities should require learners to negotiate meaning and interact meaningfully (Richards, 2006).

Based on the above account, the idea of authenticity appears many times with regard to both authenticity of materials and authenticity of the tasks employed in the classroom. It would be wise to leap back to the developing materials part and work on it to prepare authentic materials as much as possible for the activities, which is also an obvious implication gained in the review of literature on language teaching and also in the needs assessment conducted for the purposes of this study. You may refer to the literature chapter of this work for more information about the use of authentic materials. In order to reach authentic materials, you may use the internet for online magazines, forums, newspaper articles, videos and so on and may also use the printed sources such as books, newspapers and brochures.

In talking about the guidelines for the teaching methods of the FCS, the curriculum requires a communicatively oriented approach. Communicative language teaching focuses on language for meaningful communication as opposed to a focus on grammatical competence. Meaning and fluency are viewed more important than accuracy. Errors could be tolerated if the message is intelligible for the hearer (Richards & Rogers, 1986). The following briefly discusses the implications of the Communicative Language Teaching for classroom use (Richards, 2006).

- Collaborative creation of meaning is important, which leads teachers to organize pair, group or whole class activities rather than individual study activities.
- Input is important for students as it is through inputs that the students could find a starting point to develop their all language skills in that they not only develop reading and grammar but also develop communication

and speaking based upon the given input. Thus, there is a need for materials to be used as inputs.
- Linking of language skills in teaching is important just as they are usually and naturally integrated in the real world.
- Teachers should strive to use real world or authentic sources as much as possible as the basis for classroom learning.

4.2.8.1 Learner roles

Learners should be comfortable with being engaged in cooperative activities (rather than individualistic ones), working with others in pair or group work conditions, and with taking the responsibility of their own learning (Richards, 2006). Teachers should view the learners "as a negotiator between the self, the learning process and the object of learning (Richards & Rogers, 1986, p. 77).

4.2.8.2 Teacher roles

Teachers should assume the roles of facilitators, researchers, needs analysts and group process managers. Rather than being a checker for correct speech, the main responsibility of the teacher is to prepare an environment in which students may produce language for their communication and communicative purposes.

4.2.8.3 The roles of instructional materials

There is a push for the use of authentic materials. Teachers should strive to use real world or authentic sources as much as possible as the basis for classroom learning because real communication is arrived at through the use of real-life materials (Clarke & Silbertstein, 1977). For a discussion on the use of authentic materials, consult the literature review section of this work (see Chapter 2).

4.2.8.4 Instructional activities to be used

We have compiled the following list based on Richards (2006).

Real world tasks (task based-instruction)

A communicative approach stands for the inclusion of the type of activities which reflect real uses of language and approximate real-life activities (e.g. role-plays in which students are asked to practice a real-life-like role).

Information gathering activities

These activities may require students to collect information (via surveys, interviews etc.) by using their own linguistic and communicative repertoires.

Opinion-sharing activities

They refer to such types of activities in which students are invited to compare values, opinions and beliefs.

Information-transfer activities

They refer to such types of activities in which students are asked to reconstruct what they have learned and reflect it into some other format than the original one.

Reasoning-gap activities

In these activities, students are invited to make inferences and reasoning so as to arrive at new insights and information from what information has been provided to them.

Role-plays

They refer to such types of activities in which students are assigned different roles and students are required to act a scene based on the information or guidelines provided to them.

4.2.9 Planning Evaluation and an Evaluation Plan for the FSC

The evaluation plan for the FSC centers on two types of evaluation, an evaluation of students' achievement in relation to learning and the evaluation of the course in terms of its effectiveness in helping students learn. In other words, with the first question, we plan to assess the language learning of the students and with the second one we attempt to evaluate the course itself.

4.2.9.1 Course evaluation

A course evaluation questionnaire can be designed to elicit information regarding the intended learning outcomes of the course, course content and materials, course conduct and course assessment procedures. Erozan's (2005) study and her evaluation instruments can be taken as examples for evaluation purposes. This information, when supported by the data from the interviews to be performed with students and data from classroom observations, may provide information on the effectiveness of the course. Teachers may ask their colleagues to observe their classes (e.g. peer observation of the teachers' classes) or when this is not feasible, they may provide their own insights about the course conduct and teaching-learning process.

4.2.9.2 Student evaluation

We tried to envision the evidence of *main effects* and *side effects* for the FSC. As our ILOs have been basically derived from certain skills that the students are expected to develop during the course, the degree to which students are able to perform these skills are considered as evidences of main effects. The following provides an example.

- *ILO:* Students will be able to take part in discussions and debates on various topics included in the activities of a unit about the targeted topic areas.
- *Evidence for accomplishing the skill*: Students take part in discussions and debates as required by the course work.

In talking about the possible side (unintended) effects, they may have poor reading and listening skills, difficulty with understanding the authentic text or boredom with some of the themes. Based on such predictions and the needs assessment data, the following assessment plan for student evaluation was formulated.

4.2.9.2.1   FSC Class evaluation plan

This is how the students will be assessed during the semester (*The idea for the evaluation was taken and adapted from Graves, 2000, p. 221). The key idea should be the incorporation of formative assessment (i.e. evaluation of what students do during the course) and incorporation of all of what they do in the class time. The following presents a suggestion based on Graves' (2000) ideas on evaluation plans.

What	How	Percent of grade
Attendance	Daily count	5 %
Participation	Classroom observation	10%
Coursework		
Speaking Activities	Going one step by further speaking tasks	15%

What	How	Percent of grade
Presentations	Putting it all together tasks (group and individual)	15%
Midterm Exam	Oral Assessment about a given topic (when input provided)	15%
Recycling Assignments (Writing etc.)	Written Assessment	10 %
Final Exam	Presentation and oral assessment based on the presentation performed	30%

1. Attendance: There are 56 hours (14*4) of class time in a semester. When students only miss two classes, they will get an A.
   A 56 – 48 (2 absences)   C 39 – 32 (6 absences)
   B 47 – 40 (4 absences)   D 31- (7 or more absences)
2. Participation: Students' participation grade is based on the following scheme of standards.
   5   * does all of the class work and assignments
       * always motivated to speak and learn English
       * always uses only English in class
       * often takes an active part in class activities
       * performs and functions very well in pair and group work activities
   4   * does most of the classwork and assignments
       * usually motivated to speak and learn English
       * usually speaks only English in class
       * usually takes an active part in class activities
       * performs and functions well in pair and group work activities
   3   * does some of the classwork and assignments
       * sometimes motivated to speak and learn English
       * sometimes speaks English in class
       * occasionally takes an active part in class activities
       * performs and functions OK in pair and group work activities
   2   * does only a little of the classwork and assignments
       * hardly ever motivated to speak and learn English
       * rarely speaks English in class.
       * rarely takes an active part in class activities
       * does not perform and function well in pairs and group work activities
   1   * does none of the classwork and assignments
       * almost never motivated to speak and learn English
       * almost never speaks English in class
       * almost never takes an active part in class activities
       * does not perform and function very well in pairs and group work activities

5. Unit and Lesson Plan

5.1 Unit Plan

5.1.1 Rationale

Learners of the course already gained a certain degree of proficiency in English via their preparation program offered for almost 700 instruction hours in the previous year. It now seems imperative that the study of further speaking and communication skills should begin onwards to provide the students with the necessary survival skills they need to manage English language as a medium of instruction (for at least 30 % of the courses offered in their main faculty curricula). Moreover, these students need to have good speaking skills in order to cope with the communication demands of daily and work life that the students are facing/are to face with. Throughout this sample unit designed here in this chapter, it is aimed that students should gain the required speaking skills for effective communication and also for making oral presentations (not that much academic presentations, but ability to speak before an audience). Their practice with speaking skills will become more meaningful and valuable as they begin to relate it to the world beyond the school. To achieve this, the use of real-life materials and tasks are highlighted in the unit.

5.1.2 Introduction

The two-week unit is designed to further develop learners' speaking skills with the use of the other remaining main language skills as a springboard. To this end, the unit (also the whole course) follows a system in which four skills of language, speaking, listening, writing and reading are integrated to create further speaking opportunities for the learners. Speaking skills being the main focus of the unit is generated or completed through the help of listening, reading and writing activities. In this sense, reading and listening activities (i.e. receptive activities) serve as comprehensible input for the learners pushing the learners to produce the language mainly in speaking and also in writing. It is assumed that students already exhibit a certain degree of language proficiency and thus possess the basics of what and how of a language, basic sentence structure, knowledge of form, meaning and learning strategies, certain degrees of excellence in all four skills of speaking, listening, reading and writing. The four strands of language, meaning-focused input (via reading and listening activities), meaning-focused output and fluency activities (speaking and writing activities) and lastly language-focused learning (pronunciation and explanations for grammar only when needed) is also touched upon in the unit as is in fact the system to follow for the whole course.

5.1.3 Sequence

There is one obvious sequence choice: *begin with input, work forward with speaking,* and *rework it through writing.* To this end, this unit encompasses four main strands respectively: *getting started* (input), *going one step further by speaking* (output), *putting it all together* (output) and *recycling it in another form* (output). Other sequences are not offered in that to practice speaking students need something to get started and warmed up for the things to come. However, it could be possible to skip some of the activities within the strands or decrease the time spent for them depending on the pace and proficiency of the students in the skills (ILOs) specified for the activities.

5.1.4 Instructional foci

Debate, oral reconstructions, role-play, authentic and adapted reading texts, listening texts.

5.1.5 ILOs

By the end of this unit, students will be able to:

- listen for specific information in a given listening text.
- listen for the main idea in a given listening text.
- read for the main idea in a given reading text.
- read for specific information in a given reading text.
- scan for the required piece of information in a given reading text.
- identify different opinions in reading and speaking.
- evaluate different viewpoints in reading and speaking.
- make connections between ideas in reading and speaking.
- expand vocabulary and activate the passive vocabulary in their minds.
- synthesize information in a given text and natural communication.
- paraphrase the required piece of information.
- write a reaction/response paragraphs/short essays about a given topic.
- give an oral reconstruction of the information presented to them.
- give an oral response to their interlocutors.
- react to an idea presented to them.
- reflect on an idea presented to them.
- express opinions (agreement and disagreement) any topic and event.

- take part in discussions and debates on various topics.
- use correct pronunciation of common problem sounds when speaking.
- use appropriate transitions and signposts in speaking.
- deliver a speech/presentation for a given topic.
- build speaking confidence through making practice in speaking.
- adjust language to spoken discourse as needed.

5.1.6 General teaching strategies

The Communicative Language Teaching approach is required to enhance the speaking skills that are the main focus of the unit and the whole course designed. The unit is based upon the idea that language is for communication, and communication is for language, which leads itself into a communicative way of teaching. Among the process-based communicative language teaching approaches, content-based teaching approach is emphasized in that the unit designed as a sample here revolves around one theme, that is, art and four skills of language is weaved together into this thematic unit. Task-based instruction is performed with the use of opinion-sharing and information-gathering activities, role-plays and problem-solving tasks.

Following the four main strands, the teacher makes an introduction to the topic via the help of quotes from famous people, which is the warm-up stage so as to make the students acquainted with the topic of art to be covered in the remainder of the unit. Following this introduction to the topic part, the teacher leads reading and listening activities as types of pre-speaking activities in that the purpose is to provide the context for the speaking tasks to follow. These pre-speaking activities serve as the starting points for the students to generate ideas on and to get familiarized with the topic of the unit. After the getting started strand, the next strand of the unit, going one step further by speaking takes place, and this time the teacher leads the students in the communicative and task-based activities that are formed around the theme of art again, but this time takes the theme from different perspectives. Engaged with the major speaking tasks of the unit, students work in groups. It is at the end of this major speaking activity that the teacher checks and deals with linguistic problems, such as pronunciation and problematic sounds s/he has realized in class.

5.1.7 Unintended learning outcomes

There may be a few students who have poorer reading and skills compared to the others and this may be a problem for the flow of the lessons. This problem (if any) can be combated with paying more attention to the sub-skills of these major skills so that the students will be able to practice how to better deal with the texts and gain the necessary skills to better understand the reading texts.

5.1.8 Evaluation

Throughout the unit the teacher will note individuals' contributions to class discussions and their contributions and performance within their groups for the speaking and discussion activities. The presentations assigned at the end of the major speaking activities, and required to be presented following the two-week thematic unit, will be treated as test conditions to evaluate students' progress in speaking skills.

5.2 Lesson Plan

The following present the lesson plan we prepared on the theme of art and for the purposes of one of the strands.

Unit: Art

Strand: Getting One Step Further by Speaking

Course: Further Speaking Skills

Trainer: ……………..

Classroom size: 15-20 students

Level: Intermediate

Time allotted: 50 min +50 min (2 class hours)

Date: ……………..

Topic of the Lesson: Stolen Property or Finders Keepers?

Teaching aims: cultivating critical thinking, developing speaking skills

Instructional Foci : authentic reading texts about historical artifacts, a newspaper excerpt (see Appendix I for the reading passages)

Intended Learning Outcomes

By the end of the lesson, students will be able to:
- read for the main idea.
- read for specific information.
- identify different opinions.
- evaluate different viewpoints.
- express opinions (for agreement and disagreement).
- take part in discussions and debates on various topics.

(* T: teacher & Sts: Students)

Induction/Introduction/Ice breaking :

The T invites students to brainstorm about the other types of art than the art of painting they have got familiarized in the earlier parts of the lesson. (*The T may make draw a graphic organizer on the board).

Methodology

- Once the T can elicit the answer "historical artifacts (artworks) or a connotation of it", the T asks the class to briefly discuss the ownership of the artworks in that some priceless art works around the world are not now in their country of origin. Some were obtained by other countries from the origin countries through outright theft or during the war times (*students may be invited to give examples they know)
- After the above short introduction, the T invites students to read a new excerpt which will act as an introduction to the task to come (pre-speaking activity)
- The T then leads into the task for which the students will work in small groups (4 students for each group is the ideal one).
- The task is working on individual cases of historical artifacts assigned by the T randomly. There are five relevant articles about the five cases of artifacts that are not displayed in their country of origin now.
- The T talks to the groups generally about the content of the tasks (*The T may prepare a handout (i.e. paper of task requirements) for it.
- For this task, students will act as professional investigators and each in the group will have separate tasks to fulfill. The T assigns the role cards (historian, lawyer, artist and museum curator/appraiser; see Appendix J for the activity handout) that show the responsibilities of each investigator. Each investigator finds the relevant information for their role from the articles provided by the T. When each group member complete their part of the task, the groups come together to prepare a presentation to the Court of Public Opinion (the whole class) demonstrating their final decision about the fate of the artifact. To this end, they need to take a position about the fate of the artwork: *Will it stay in the current place or country, or will it be returned to the country which it originally belongs to?*
- Student Presentation: the groups present their case to the whole class (i.e. the Court of Public Opinion).
- Evaluation of the Court of Public Opinion (the whole class): they evaluate the groups' presentations and give the final decision about the fate of the artworks.
- Follow-up Task: *Discussion Questions* (The T may guide the discussion as a whole-class activity or as a pair-work followed by a whole class activity)
  - How important are the stories of the artworks? Should we learn about their ancient stories to understand these works more properly?

- What could be the conditions for artworks to be taken from their origin countries (as spoils of war, theft etc.)? Which of these cases makes the misplacement of artworks more acceptable or less acceptable from a moral point of view?
- What should countries do protect their historical artworks?

Assessment

- As a suggestion for what may follow the role-play and follow-up discussion activity, the T may ask the students to write on the graphic organizer provided in a T chart format: *Reasons why artifacts should be returned? & Reasons why artifacts should not be returned?*
- After this brief summary with reasons, the T may provide another discussion question: What policy do you think Turkey should follow about the artifacts that were either looted, given away as presents or lost due to some other reasons like war, lack of interest, and protection? (* At this stage, the T may evaluate learners' progress in terms of expressing opinions for agreement and disagreement and their understanding of the spoken outputs (discussion earlier).
- Pronunciation: The T may also deal with the problematic sounds (i.e. the sounds that the students are having difficulty in pronouncing) which s/he has recognized during the activities previously performed. (*The T may use the pronunciation info & exercises box to gain some material to deal with the students' problematic sounds).

(*If a vital need arises for the grammar, the T may briefly talk about it).

Closure

Based on the responses of learners on the graphic organizer-based questions and the final discussion question relevant to Turkey, the T summarizes the lesson.

Assignment

- The T talks about and assigns the next week's homework for the Putting it all together strand, that is, a presentation activity in which sts are asked to find a news item about art and to present it before the class. The T gives the details about the activity (*The T may prepare a handout (paper of presentation requirements) for it).

6. Field Testing of the Unit Plan

The unit plan we devised was put into practice by a teacher we provided training for the implementation of the unit in line with the curriculum approach and framework. Both formal and informal ways of eliciting feedback about the unit in specific and the curriculum in general were employed.

Formal information was elicited by means of classroom observation form used by one of the researchers of this book during the class time that the teacher put our designed lesson plan into practice. That is, one of the researchers was in the class observing the teacher. We used the classroom observation form devised by Erozan (2005). Another data were gathered by means of the feedback sheet administered to the students. The feedback sheet was designed based on two main inquiries, *strengths* and *weaknesses* of the activity performed in the class. Therefore, students were asked to write about their ideas of the lesson on the relevant columns labeled as strengths and weakness. The following themes and codes were derived as the result of the thematic analyses of the data collected via the feedback sheets.

Strengths

Strengths in relation to practice in the class

- Engagement with drawing a visual form of the artwork
- Satisfaction with the group work
- Brainstorming in the group work atmosphere

Strengths in relation to material (input) and topic used

- Conformity in the pieces of the same-topic materials
- Interesting topic covered in the materials
- Enjoyable topic covered in the materials
- Real-life relevance of the topic covered in the materials

Strengths in relation to strategies/skills developed through the activity

- Guessing the meaning of unknown words from the context
- Employing research skills to seek information about the art works

Weaknesses

Weaknesses in relation to the material (input)

- The presence of a lot of unknown words
- Loaded content of the reading texts

In looking at the results, though the positives about the activity conducted surpass the negatives, it would be wise to consider them for a better implementation of the further units of this course designed for future practice. The presence of unknown lexis and loaded content are the two main characteristics of the authentic materials. The reading passages used as the input in this study have not been simplified based on the idea that students could cope with them as the teacher would guide them to try for a partial understanding of the texts, total comprehension is not sought. However, the literature presents contrasting views on that point. Widdowson (1996, 1998), for example, claims that simplified passages are valuable as the original ones as it is the procedure employed that is making something authentic not the material used itself. He recommends simplification of the authentic materials for their use with students exhibiting lower levels of proficiency in English. For the purposes of my own course, as the students are expected to ve those who have completed a-year-preparatory program in English composed of almost 700 hours of instruction, authentic texts were decided to be used as they were. Moreover, there would be a prequisite to take the Further Speaking Skills in that a successful completion of the preperatory school at the upper-intermediate level is required. Thus, the students registered into this course will be expected to exhibit higher levels of proficiencies. However, when a teacher experiences difficulty with the use of authentic texts that are seemingly posing problems to students' understanding, they may opt to simplify them. Though the simplification of the authentic texts is debatable in the literature, the teacher may try it very sensitively by use of very brief and small simplifications. The difficulty reported by the students in understanding the texts due to unknown vocabulary items and loaded content during the field-test course may have stemmed from the fact that these students have not been accustomed to work with such type of an input in their courses, which has been also worded by the teacher putting the lesson we designed into practice. The teacher told me that the students worked on purely authentic texts perhaps for the first time in the course of their English study and this very first experience might have them feel anxious for the thorough understanding of the texts. However, when she made a further explanation that the aim is not a complete comprehension but a partial one (just briefly getting the basic answers to the questions posed for the roles-historian, museum appraiser, artist and lawyer), the students tried to better cope with the text employing the strategy of guessing the meanings of unknown words from the context.

Formal information was also collected through the observation performed by one of the researchers of this book within the class during the two class hours allocated for the field-testing of the lesson plan. The observation instrument helped the researcher to take notes in relation to several themes, teacher behaviors, student behaviors, input (the material) used and the tasks/activities observed. The following themes and codes were composed from the notes taken on the observation form.

Teacher behaviors during the activity

- Teacher as a guide
- Teacher as a linguistic assistant

Student behaviors during the activity

Good points

- Motivation and zest in reading the texts
- Motivation and zest in task of producing a visual form of the artwork
- Motivation and interest in the topic, artworks

Problems

- Students' difficulty in understanding the reading text
- Lack of cultural knowledge

Input (materials)

- Lexical density of the reading passages
- Interesting topic provided in reading passages
- Length of the reading passages

Once the teacher implementing the designed lesson plan set the scene for the activity, she acted like a guide moving in class from one group to another during the reading activity. For some complaints about the lexical density and length of the reading passages, she was again guiding students to understand the passages partially by discouraging their tendency for a complete understanding of the whole passage. Some students seemed really having difficulties in understanding the passages and they insistently ask the help of the teacher. The teacher needed to spend more individual time with these students, which in turn confirm our assigning a prerequisite of proficiency level to take this course. Though students seem to finish a whole year program in English and are expected to graduate with an upper-intermediate level of English proficiency, not all students might reach to that level. Students looked motivated to learn more about the artworks told in the reading passages, by saying to each other " How could they carry it to that country?" and "Why can't we ask it back? It is our property". One of the students uttered "I am not very into museums and this type of intellectual activities, but I liked these misplaced things", which shows that the topic of art was interesting to them. Another good point about the activity was the act of drawing a representation or a visual form of the artifacts discussed. Not only had the responsible role, the illustrator of the group, but also the other group members made their contributions to the visual product to use in their presentations. In our opinion, it kept students engaged mentally and physically in that they could reflect upon their understanding of the artwork in relation to its characteristics and also in relation to its history. Students could not differentiate the roles from one another, for example, they frequently asked what a museum appraiser does, and what its difference is from the duty of the historian. This may be due to the students' lack of cultural knowledge, and therefore, the teacher may spend some more time explaining the duties of the roles given and answer the students' questions regarding the roles. In looking back to the whole activity, the teacher talk was less than the student talk in the classroom and students were active by asking their peers about the unknown vocabulary items, drawing the visual form for the presentation and discussing and reflecting on the artworks as a group.

We, the researchers, gained some *informal information* from teacher putting our lesson into practice. She recommended that the teacher should set the scene for the activity in a very effective way for the further conduct of the activity. As her students were not very much used to that type of activities during their study, they felt somehow awkward at the very beginning. Therefore, she recommended that perhaps at the very first lessons of your speaking curriculum, the teachers should explain about activity to come, but she also mentioned that once the students are used to such activities, the need for the guidance of the teacher would be at minimums. Another recommendation was about the roles given for the activity. Though students know most of the roles, the role of museum appraiser was not that obvious to them. Therefore, she recommended more explanation for the meaning and responsibilities of this role. She further recommended that some of the questions posed to the roles needed some changes with regard to their wording. She also realized that students work better with direct questions compared to indirect ones. As is also mentioned earlier, the teacher realized students' complains about the difficulty and length of the reading texts. However, she also mentioned that the students found a way out as they tried, and in spite of their complaints, she observed that their motivation is high. She gave an example of one of her students saying "it was nice to see that with our modest English, we were able to achieve such a compelling text and it is a very nice feeling". Though we designed our study ideally for 20 students, her class was 22 in size. The teacher creatively dispersed two historians for some of the groups to solve the class size problem. It also made sense to me in that in the texts offer a lot of information about the history of the artwork so that two historians would not be in excess.

As another positive side of the activity, the teacher mentioned the group work performance. She reported students enjoying the group work atmosphere created for the sake of the activity. The students liked the idea of working individually first to collect information for their specific roles and then later coming together to generate a holistic opinion and decision as a group. In the two class hours allocated for the lesson we designed, only two of the groups could perform their presentations to the court of public opinion (i.e. the whole class), and the remaining three groups were left to the next class. Therefore, as one of the researchers also observed and as the teacher recommended it the time needs to be extended for the activity. Perhaps the reason for this could be the length of the reading passages. Thus, as a piece of suggestion for future practice, it appears that more time will be needed in class when long reading passages will be used as inputs.

7. Discussion

7.1 Comments on the Process and Design

When we look back at the work we have done in this project, we see a lot of positives about the design model we employed. Much of the literature about curriculum design portrays this process as a linear and step-by-step process in which you start with the needs assessment procedures and based on the results of needs assessment you formulate objectives, determine content and so on. However, based on our experiences as teachers, we feel it that course development or more specifically lesson preparation and planning does not work in that way. For example, when we made a plan of the next day's class, we usually move back and forth between our decisions about the material to select, the instructional techniques to use and the objectives we set for this lesson. Therefore, for this project, we wanted to devise an instructional model which is non-linear and flexible. Flexibility is the key word for our instructional model, and we think, this is a strength of this model in that the flexibility or opportunity to start the course design process at any point the course designers would like to prefer gives the course designers some autonomy and freedom resulting in making more informed and meaningful decisions. The decisions pertaining to where to start course design in fact mostly relates to the course designers' own beliefs about teaching and learning and also to the contextual characteristics and the conditions of the course to be designed. Furthermore, as Larsen-Freeman (1997) also puts forth, there is a non-linear and organic way of learning. If the learning is defined in that way, why do we choose a linear model to facilitate this process? By following a non-linear model, you (the teacher) do not have the feeling that you are skipping something or doing something wrong, which is often a sort of feeling we have with the linear and rational models. Moreover, you cannot be always clear about a process or a component of your course when you first start your instructional planning. However, as you proceed to the other components you gain more insights, with these new insights you may come back to an earlier step to revise it.

Another strength of the model relates to the foundational steps guiding the following procecesses and actions in the model. These two foundational procecesses, *articulating beliefs* and *defining context* were particularly placed at the very bottom of the graphical representation of the model because of the guiding and leading functions assigned to them. For example, it would be impossible for a teacher to choose a teaching method that is contradictory to his or her thinking about the nature of language learning. In the same sense, it would be unwise for a teacher to decide about content that his or her students would not be interested in, or to choose an instructional strategy integrated with technology when his or her resources are technologically limited.

From the above account about the course design model, it would be wise to feel that course development is always a work in progress. In line with the idea of this continuing progress, our model centers on process described with verbs (gerund format) and these verbs delineate that course design is a continuing thinking process in which course designers are involved in some detailed thinking and reasoning before they arrive at any decision about the course to be designed. They form a coherent and meaningful course plan as a result of this reasoning and logical thinking process.

The model we devised has two components regarding content determination corresponding to the only one content determination component found in most course design models in the literature. There are two components entitled *conceptualizing content* and *organizing content*. We see it advantageous again since conceptualization of content leads you to the organization of content with more confidence. Therefore, this two-step process for content determination helps course designers to make more informed and confident decisions about content selection by spending more time on thinking about all of the necessary details of course content to be offered to learners.

Materials development acts like a starting point for content determination. In this essence, the key idea behind the determination of content in my course is the selection of instructional foci that will shape my content organization. This model guides course designers to consider the process of developing materials and determination of unit content together. This collobaration between determination of materials and content is meaningful in that instructional activities and the materials to be utilized often precede the determination of content (Posner & Rudnitsky, 1997). That is, materials (e.g. texts or videos) the teachers like and find appropriate to use in a course, can simply form the course content. This also depicts a backward-desing approach in contrast to the forward and hierarchial designing process of most models in the literature in which course designers or teachers are required to choose materials after they determine the content. However, in this model, course designers or teachers have the freedom to move from materials to form their course content.

The evaluation part of our model proposes two types of assessment, student assessment and course assessment and we think this is feasible because course evaluation adds a lot to the course development. The student assessment attempts to include all the course work, that is, what is covered in the lesson is put into test so that we can understand how much all the components of the course are working. For the course assessment, we propose it to be performed around the four components of a course, objectives, course content and materials, course conduct and course assessment procedures, which, we think is quite logical to take into consideration. Without an evaluation of all the course components, it would not be wise to discuss the success of this course.

Another positive about our model is the incorporation of field testing or teaching part. Though our model fits into the planning the course phase of the course development cycle, we think testing the effectiveness of the parts of the course (one unit at least) we designed will contribute to our plan, and without putting it into use, you cannot see the actual learning outcomes. However, we put this component outside the course planning arc as it goes into the teaching the course cycle. In this way, it could be optional for some teachers who have no opportunities to field test the unit they have prepared, which again is an indicator of the flexibility idea behind our course design process. With regard to the application of this model in the arena of English language teaching, we think it really fits into the nature of language learning which itself is in fact unpredictable and non-linear.

For the things that could be done to improve this curriculum for future practice, we would suggest the designers to prepare some guidelines for the selection of instructional content which will provide more linkage between the instructional foci selected (content), instructional strategies and ILOs so that those using our model could understand the main gist of the speaking course design. The gist here is non-dependence to any fixed coursebook or material. The gist is choosing which material would be more suitable to your ILOs and the techniques you want to use. Through these instructional foci, you determine your content, that is, the instructional foci become your content, the vehicle for you have your students achieve the ILOs of the course. In this context, as is the case with the unpredictable nature of speaking and communication in the real world, the speaking course do not set out with clear frames. Therefore, we would suggest to those who want to take this curriculum further to be careful about the selection of instructional foci around which they will build their lessons.

In talking about the weaknesses of our model, though we feel positive about it, we would consider those teachers who want to see step-by-step guidelines to follow. Some field-dependent minded teachers will feel awkward with this type of a flexible model. These teachers may also feel uncomfortable with the free choice of instructional foci. That is why, we suggested above the provision of some guidelines on the selection and use of instructional foci. For those teachers who are constrained by some rules such as choice of a specific book or a source at their institutions, this model may not be working.

Though it is not a weakness, we think this model could not be applicable to all courses. For example, the use of the model in technical courses may not be practical and meaningful in that in these courses, each and every step should be controlled from the very beginning by means of a step-by-step planned procedure for course development so as to protect all involved stakeholders from any possible harm. For instance, for the implementation stage of a technical course where students are required to use a machine or a piece of equipment, every previous step should be carefully designed following a certain route of required activities so that there will be no harm to these students when they are dealing with the machines during course implementation.

In talking about our last words on this project, we feel that this project is always a work in progress as the nature of course design is itself and the real outcomes are seen when the planned course here is put into real practice. We think only that time we will be able to better see the weaknesses and strengths and the degree to which the intended learning outcomes are transferred into actual learning outcomes.

7.2 Suggestions for Further Course Design Work

Course design may seem complicated or difficult to some teachers or practitioners. However, when performed with the help of a guiding schema or model, course design work may be organized, meaningful and easy to employ for those attempting to design a course. For the purposes of language teaching, it is known that teaching and learning languages differ from the teaching and learning of other disciplines. These differences can be particularly seen in terms of determination of content, selection of teaching methods and techniques and even in terms of assessment practices. In this essence, non-linear, unpredictable and organic nature and capacity of learning languages (Larsen-Freeman, 1997) also requires a non-linear and authentic procedures and methods to teach them. Therefore, those aiming to design a language course may use this exemplary work reported in this book as a guide for their own courses to be designed. However, the model can be also used to design courses other than languages based on the assumption that linear and hierarchical nature and methods of most other disciplines have been replaced by more flexible, student-centered outlooks of today. Accordingly, the course design model and process described in this book is believed to give some insights to couse designers and teachers about designing courses in many discipline areas.

Although the course design process and the utilization of the model have been described in detail in this book, only one lesson plan have been developed and practiced as a part of the FSC curriculum. In order to compensate for this limitation, the writers aimed to provide the readers with a detailed descriptions and explanations of the course design process they were recommending in this book. Therefore, the design steps and procedures described in detail in Chapter 4 and later put into practice in Chapter 5 can be used to develop the further units of the FSC curriculum. It should be also remembered that without the actual field-testing of the designed units, the course design would be imcomplete. That is, field-testing help course designers to see the weaknesses and problems prior to the real utilization of the whole curriculum. In this regard, field-testing procedures equal to a pilot study, which you will remember from most research studies. Without a pilot study, it is known that the validity and reliability of the research study and the intruments used in this research would be affected negatively. In summary, field testing of the following units should be performed prior to the real utilization of the developed curricula and for this project, the readers are recommended to read Chapter 4 and Chapter 5 in detail.

References

Bawcom, L. (1995). Designing an advanced speaking course. *English Teaching Forum. 33*(1). 41-43.

Brown, G. & Yule, G. (1983). *Teaching the spoken language*. Cambridge: Cambridge University Press.

Brown, G. (1995). *Elements of language curriculum: A systematic approach to program development*. Boston: Heinle& Heinle.

Burns, A. (1998). Teaching speaking. *Annual Review of Applied Linguistics. 18*, 102-123.

Canale, M. & Swain, M. (1980). Theoretical bases of communicative approaches to second language teaching and testing. *Applied Linguistics, 1*(1), 1-47.

Canale, M. (1983). From communicative competence to language pedagogy. In J. Richards & J. Schmidt (Eds.), *Language and Communication* (pp. 2-27). London: Longman.

Clark, M., & Silberstein, S. (1977). Toward a realization of psycholinguistic principles in the ESL reading class. *Language Learning, 21*(1), 48-65.

Dubin, F., & Olshtain, E. (1986). *Course design: Developing programs and materials for language learning*. Cambridge: Cambridge University Press.

Ellis, R. (1990). *Instructed second language acquisition*. Oxford: Blackwell Publishing.

Erozan, F. (2005). *Evaluating the language improvement courses in the undergraduate ELT curriculum at Eastern Mediterranean University: A case study*. Unpublished doctoral dissertation, Middle East Technical University, Ankara.

Graves, K. (2000). *Designing language courses*. Boston, MA: Heinle & Heinle.

Gilmore, A. (2007). Authentic materials and authenticity in foreign language learning. *Language Teaching. 40*(2), 97–118.

Guariento, W. & Morley, A. (2001). Text and task authenticity in the EFL classroom. *ELT Journal, 55* (4), 347-352.

Hongyan, Y. (n.d.). A learner-centered curriculum of speaking class for non-English majors. Retrieved from http://www.celea.org.cn/pastversion/lw/pdf/Yang%20Hongyan.pdf

Jiayan, G. & Jianbin, H. (2010). On communicative competence in curriculum design: A comparison of the college English curriculum requirements and the English curriculum standards. *Polyglossia, 18*, 73-86.

Krashen (1981). Second language acquisition and second language learning. Retrieved from http://www.sdkrashen.com/SL_Acquisition_and_Learning/index.html

Krashen, S.D. (1982). Principles and practice in second language acquisition. Retrieved from http://www.sdkrashen.com/Principles_and_Practice/index.html.

Larsen-Freeman, D. (1997). Chaos/complexity: Science and second languge acquisition. *Applied Linguistics, 18* (2), 141-165.

Mager, R.F. (1975). Preparing instructional objectives. (2nd ed.). Belmont, CA: Fearon.
McCarthy, M. (1991) *Discourse analysis for language teachers*. Cambridge: Cambridge University Press.
Morrow, K. (1977). Authentic texts and ESP. In S. Holden (Ed.), English for Specific Purposes (pp. 13-17). London: Modern English Publications.
Nunan, D. (1988). *Syllabus design*. Oxford: Oxford University Press.
Nation, I. S. P. & Macalister, J. (2010). Language Curriculum Design. New York & London: Routledge.
Posner, G. J. & Rudnitsky, A. N. (1997). *Course design: A guide to curriculum development for teachers*. New York: Longman.
Richards, J.C. (1990). The Language teaching matrix. New York: Cambridge University Press.
Richards, J. C. (2006). *Communicative language teaching today*. New York: Cambridge University Press.
Richards, J.C., & Rodgers, T. S. (1986). *Approaches and methods in language teaching*. Cambridge: Cambridge University Press.
Slade, D. & Thornbury, S. (2006). Conversation: From description to pedagogy. Cambridge: Cambridge University Press.
Stern, H. H. (1992). Issues and options in language teaching. Oxford: Oxford University Press.
Yalden, J. (1987). *Principles of course design for language teaching*. Cambridge: Cambridge University Press.
Yel, A. (2009). *Evaluation of the effectiveness of English courses in Sivas Anatolian High Schools*. Unpublished master's thesis, Middle East Technical University, Ankara.
Widdowson, H. G. (1979). *Explorations in applied linguistics*. Oxford: Oxford University Press.
Widdowson, H. G. (1996). Comment: authenticity and autonomy in ELT. *ELT Journal 50*(1), 67–68.
Widdowson, H. G. (1998). Context, community, and authentic language. *TESOL Quarterly. 32* (4), 705–716.

Appendices

Appendix A

List of Activities

(Suggested by Bawcow, 1995, p.41)

- acting out role plays
- analyzing a problem
- brainstorming
- convincing someone to buy something
- critical assessment of books, plays, TV programs and movies
- debating
- describing people
- describing personal experiences: embarrassing, frightening, or funny situations, dreams
- describing a process
- designing publicity campaigns
- explaining the location of a place or object initiating conversations
- interviewing: personal questions, hypothetical questions
- informing someone about your country for alphabetical ordering
- jigsaw listening, reading and making commercials
- making impromptu speeches
- making presentations
- planning projects: a commune, educational institute, expedition
- ranking: (qualities, jobs,)
- retelling a story, summarizing
- seeking advice: polls, surveys
- talking about events,
- telling a story from another person's point of view
- writing dialogs, skits and plays'

Appendix B

Writing Activity Sheet for Needs Assessment

Dear students,

We need your help to develop an advanced speaking course aiming at developing further the speaking skills of the students who have completed the English preparatory program in the previous year. If you had the chance to take an advanced speaking course, what expectations and aims would you have in this course? What sort of difficulties or problems are you experiencing with speaking English? The curricula to be designed in the light of your responses to the following questions will be beneficial for the students who are to take this course and the teachers who are to teach this course in the future.

Thank you for your contribution.

Ali Yıldırım & Gülçin Mutlu

Writing Activity (For Students)

1. Write about the difficulties and problems you face when speaking English

   _____
   _____
   _____

2. Write about your personal aims in and expectations from the advanced speaking course to be offered to you in your degree program here? Please also specify the three main goals you plan to achieve/reach in this speaking course below.

   _____
   _____
   _____

   The goals I want to achieve in this class (3 main goals):

   a) _____
   b) _____
   c) _____

Appendix C

Student Interviews Schedule

Introduction
1. How many hours do you take at school in a week?
2. Have you ever taken a course related to English speaking skills?
3. How many courses in your degree program are offered in English?

Questions about Content and Process
1. What are your expectations from the advanced level speaking skills course?
   Probe: Your needs to be fulfilled in the course?
   Your interests and likes that you expect this course to include/emphasize?
2. What sort of content and topics would you like to learn in this course? What sort of topics attract you in this course? Why?
   Alternative Question: What should be the main content of this course? Why?
3. What kind of activities would you like to perform in this class? Why?
   Alternative Question: In your opinion, how should the course instructor teach this course? What type of activities should be used in this course?
4. What can you tell me about your own performance in English speaking skills? How would you assess yourself in terms of your speaking skills?
   Probe: The problems experienced so far?
   Your level of proficiency in English in general?
   Your level of proficiency in speaking English?
   Your unfulfilled needs and expectations in the previously taken English courses?
5. In your opinion, how should you be assessed in the advanced level English speaking course? Why?
   Alternative Question: What kind of testing situations and tests do you like and prefer in the *speaking* course?

Appendix D

Interview Schedule with the Teachers of English

Introduction
1. How many hours of English do you teach in a week?
2. How many hours of speaking lessons do you teach now/did you teach in the previous years?
3. For how many years have you been teaching English?

Questions about Content and Process
1. What should be the main goals of an advanced level English speaking course?
2. In your opinion, what is the most crucial content that the students of the advanced speaking course are to understand, learn and develop?
    Probe: Which specific topics, concepts, ideas and perspectives?
    What sort of content?
    Alternative Question: What are your recommendations as to the topics and content to be used in the advanced speaking course?
3. What prequisite level of knowledge and skills are the students of the advanced speaking course required to possess in order to be successful in this course?
4. What sort of skills are the students of this course expected to develop and implement during and by the end of this course?
5. How can you help students gain and develop the skills you mentioned for the purposes of the previous question?
    Alternative Question: What sort of teaching activities and tasks can you develop/utilize as a teacher for the students to be successful in developing the skills aimed at in this course?
6. What are your recommendations as to the assessment of speaking skills?
    Sonda: What sort of assessment methods and procedures?
    Assessing with rubrics?
    Peer assessment?
    Quizzez, projects and portfolios?
    Alternative Question: How can you test/evaluate the extent to which the students have managed to achieve the course aims?

Appendix E

Interview Schedule for Content Teachers

Introduction

1. How many hours of English do you teach in a week?
2. How many hours a week do you teach a course in your discipline area in English?
3. For how many years have you been teaching?

Questions about Content and Process

1. What are your recommendations as to the topics, concepts, ideas and perspectives that will form the course content of the advanced speaking course?

    Alternative Question: What are your recommendations as to the topics and content to be used in the advanced speaking course?

2. What sort of topics or content attract the students in the advanced speaking course and what sort of topics or content is likely to contribute to the students' own discipline areas (i.e. content departments at the university)?
3. What difficulties and problems related to speaking levels or skills of these students do you face when you teach your area courses to them?

    Alternative Question: Do the students who have completed the English preparatory program and become eligible to take your area courses experience difficulties or problems related to speaking English in your courses, which also influences your conduct of your area course?

4. In your opinion, what should be the competencies of the students regarding speaking skills in order to start the content department courses in their particular faculties?
5. What issues or conditions should we consider when forming the objectives of this advanced speaking course?
6. What are your overall recommendations for the advanced speaking course to be offered to the freshman students in your degree program here?

Appendix F

Student Questionnaire (Bilingual Form)

Dear students,

We need your opinions for the selection of course content and determination of language skills the course will center on. Below you will find a questionnaire including two sections. You are expected to answer the questions about the course topics in the first section and language skills to be developed in the second section.

Thank you for your participation in this study.

Sevgili Öğrenciler,

Geliştirmekte olduğumuz ileri konuşma becerileri dersi için konu seçimi ve derste üzerinde durulacak dil beceriler konularında sizin düşüncelerinize ihtiyaç duymaktayız. Aşağıdaki anket 2 bölümden oluşmaktadır. I. bölümde ilginizi çekebilecek konuları, II. bölümde ise bu derste size kazandırılacak becerilerle ilgili soruları cevaplandırmanız beklenmektedir.
Katılımız için teşekkür ederiz.

Gülçin Mutlu & Ali Yıldırım

SECTION I

A. Please rate the list of given topics below using the following rating scale. (Aşağıda listelenen konuları verilen ölçeğe göre değerlendiriniz)

3 = very much interesting (çok ilgi çekici)

2 = interesting (ilgi çekici)

0 = not interesting (ilgi çekici değil)

1 = not very much interesting (çok ilgi çekici değil)

1. CRIME (justice, computers, self-defense, drugs etc.)
   SUÇ (adalet, bilgisayar, kişisel savunma, uyuşturucu madde vb)
2. ECOLOGY (pollution, energy, urban renewal, endangered species etc.)
   EKOLOJİ, DOĞA (kirlilik, enerji, kentsel yenileşme, yok olma tehlikesi ile karşı karşıya olan türler)
3. EDUCATION (problems, experience vs. academic requirements, etc.)
   EĞİTİM (sorunlar, tecrübe-akademik gereklilikler karşılaştırılması vb.)

4. ETHICS (business, euthanasia, personal relations, advertising, the media, clonned babies, abortion, terrorism, etc.)
   ETİK/AHLAK KURALLARI (iş ahlakı, ötenazi, kişisel ilşkilerde ahlak, reklamcılık sektöründe ahlak, medya, klonlanmış bebekler, kürtaj, terror vb.)
5. ETHNICITY and STEREOTYPING (cultural stereotyping, men vs. women etc.)
   ETNİK KÖKEN VE KALIPLAŞTIRMA (kültürel olarak kalıplaştırma, kadın ve erkekler olarak kalıplaştırma vb.)
6. HEALTH, FITNESS and BEAUTY (dieting, exercising, sports and appearance, etc.)
   SAĞLIK, SPOR VE GÜZELLİK (beslenme, spor yapma, spor dalları ve görünüş vb.)
7. ART (painting, music, museums etc.)
   SANAT (resim, müzik, müzeler vb.)
8. HUMAN RELATIONS (dating, marriage, children, divorce, etc.)
   İNSAN İLİŞKİLERİ (flört, evlilik, çocuklar, boşanma vb.)
9. MARKETING & MONEY (finance, gambling, fraud, consumerism, shopping and e-commerce etc.)
   SATIŞ-PAZARLAMA VE PARA (finans, kumar, dolandırıcılık, tüketim, alışveriş ve online ticaret vb.)
10. PERSONALITY (psychology, astrology, dreams, conflicts, personal traits etc.)
    KİŞİLİK (psikoloji, astroloji, rüyalar, çatışmalar, kişilik özellikleri vb.)
11. PERCEPTIONS ON AGING (retirement, taking care of the elderly, discrimination against the elderly etc.)
    YAŞLANMA ÜZERİNE GÖRÜŞLER (emeklilik, yaşlılarla ilgilenme/bakma, yaşlılara karşı ayrımcılık vb.)
12. SCIENCE & TECHNOLOGY (computers, electronics, networking – Facebook, Twitter etc., digital age, inventions, etc.)
    BİLİM VE TEKNOLOJİ (bilgisayarlar, elektronik, sosyal ağlar, dijital çağ, buluşlar vb.)
13. ENTERTAINTMENT & MEDIA (television, advertising, tv programs, newspapers etc.)
    EĞLENCE VE MEDYA (televizyon, reklamcılık, televizyon programları, gazeteler vb.)
14. TRANSPORTATION & TRAVEL (means of transportation, holidays, destinations, cities etc.)
    ULAŞIM VE SEYEHAT (ulaşım araçları/yolları, tatiller, gezilecek yerler, şehirler vb.)

15. TURKEY (cultural aspects, politics, economy, labor, music, sports, education etc.)
    TÜRKİYE (kültürel şeyler, politika, ekonomi, işçilik, müzik, spor, eğitim vb.

B. Write the numbers of the five most interesting topics for you to the space given below by choosing from the above topics numbered from 1 to 15. "1" stands for the most interesting topic)

(Yukarıda 1'den 15' e kadar numaralandırılan konulardan en çok ilgi duyduğunuz 5 tanesinin numarasını boşluklara yazınız. "1" numara en çok ilginizi çekeni göstermektedir)

C. Please write the topics that are not included in the above list but you would like to talk or discuss in the classroom.

(Yukarıda listelenmeyen fakat sizin sınıfta tartışmaktan/konuşmaktan hoşlanacağınız konular varsa lütfen aşağıya belirtiniz)

SECTION II

Rate your difficulty level and the degree of importance you feel for the following list of skills using the scale of 1 to 4 below.

(Aşağıda konuşma dersi ile ilgili verilen beceriler için sağ tarafta hissettiğiniz zorluk derecelerini, sol tarafta ise bu becerilere verdiğiniz önem derecesini 1'den 4'e uzanan ölçek üzerinde işaretleyiniz.)

(1) Not important (Önemli değil)
(2) Somewhat important (Biraz önemli)
(3) Important (Önemli)
(4) Very much important (Çok önemli)

Becerinin önem derecesi The degree of importance of the skill				Bu derste değinilecek beceriler The skills to be emphasized in this class	Yaşanan zorluk derecesi The degree of difficulty faced			
1	2	3	4		1	2	3	4
				Building confidence in speaking (Konuşmada güven hissini sağlama)				
				Choosing appropriate presentation topics (Uygun sunum konularını seçme)				
				Adjusting language to spoken discourse (Dili konuşma alanına uydurma)				
				Using the appropriate transitions and signposts (Konuşmada uygun geçiş yapılarını ve belirteçleri kullanma)				
				Expressing and supporting ideas in speaking (Konuşmada fikirlerini ifade etme ve destekleme)				
				Delivering a speech/presentation (Konuşma/sunum yapma)				
				Presenting information in an organized way (Bilgiyi düzenli bir şekilde sunma)				
				Asking and answering questions (Soru sorup cevap verme)				
				Presenting as a team (Grup olarak sunum yapma)				
				Giving and taking the floor in speaking (Konuşmada söz alıp söz verme)				
				Using basic conversational strategies in dialogues (Diyaloglarda basit konuşma stratejilerini kullanma)				
				Giving an oral reconstruction (Bir olayı yeniden yapılandırarak anlatma)				
				Giving an oral response (Sözlü olarak yanıt verme)				
				Reacting to an idea (Bir fikre karşılık/yanıt verme)				
				Reflecting on an idea (Verilen bir fikrin üzerine gidip konuşma/bir fikir üzerinde daha ayrıntılı olarak konuşma)				
				Taking part in discussions and debates on various topics (Çeşitli konulardaki tartışmalara ve müzakerelere katılma)				
				Using correct pronunciation of problem sounds (İngilizce 'de problemli olabilecek sesleri doğru olarak telaffuz etme)				
				Practicing stress and intonation patterns (İngilizcedeki uygun vurgu ve tonlama desenlerini kullanma)				

Appendix G

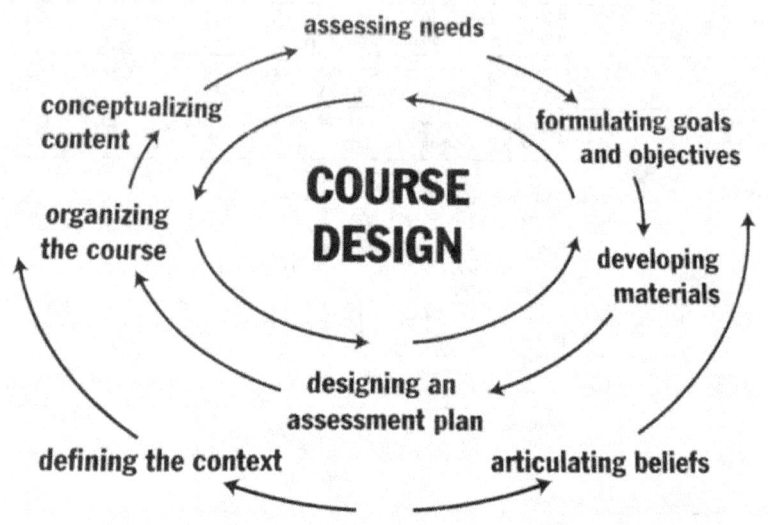

Graves' Language Course Desing Model (Source: Graves, 2000, p. 3)

Appendix H

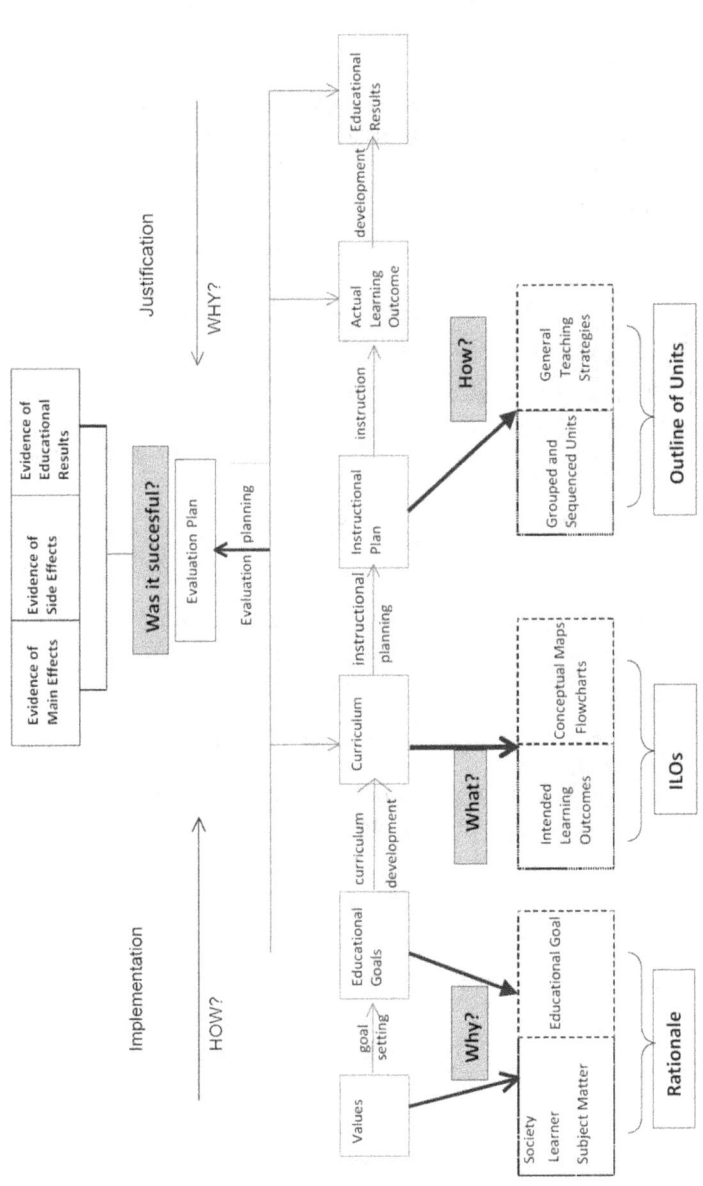

Posner & Rudnitsky Course Design Model (Source: Posner & Rudnitsky, 1997, p. 12)

Appendix I

Instructional Foci (Reading Passages) for the Unit plan

1. KohiNoor Diamond

https://www.theguardian.com/commentisfree/2016/feb/16/koh-i-noor-diamond-britain-illegally-india-pakistan-afghanistan-history-tower
https://www.ft.com/content/0f17f436-5089-11e7-bfb8-997009366969

2. The Elgin Marbles

http://www.voanews.com/content/a-13-a-2003-04-08-43-greece-66313202/542975.html
http://www.elginism.com/20040115/marbles-reunited-campaign-launch/

3. Benin Bronzes

https://www.telegraph.co.uk/news/2018/06/20/bringing-home-benin-bronzes-nigeria-open-loans-rather-permanent/
https://www.theartnewspaper.com/comment/law-restitution-and-the-benin-bronzes

4. Priam's Gold Collection

http://www.iol.co.za/scitech/technology/russia-refuses-to-give-up-trojan-treasure-1.235036
http://www.independent.co.uk/news/world/trojan-gold-fuels-rift-over-war-treasures-1305105.html)

5. Ancien Marble Head

http://www.independent.co.uk/life-style/history/turkey-demands-return-of-its-elgin-marble-2349791.html
http://articles.cnn.com/2011-09-08/world/turkey.archaeological.repatriation_1_anatolia-greek-government-marble-head?_s=PM:WORLD

Appendix J

Activity Handout for Teacher

(adapted from http://score.rims.k12.ca.us/activity/stolen/student.html)

Input: Cases and Sources for Misplaced Art

1. *KohiNoor Diamond* – It is *originally* from Punjabi, but now it is placed among the British *Royal* Crown Jewels

   News article: Koh-i-Noor: the World's Most Infamous Diamond (* to be retrieved from https://www.ft.com/content/0f17f436-5089-11e7-bfb8-997009366969)

   News article: The Koh-i-Noor diamond is in Britain illegally. But it should still stay there (* to be retrieved from https://www.theguardian.com/commentisfree/2016/feb/16/koh-i-noor-diamond-britain-illegally-india-pakistan-afghanistan-history-tower)

2. *The Elgin Marbles* – It is originally from Greece, but now exhibited in the British Museum

   News article: Greece Repeats Demand for Return of Elgin Marbles (* to be retrieved from http://www.voanews.com/content/a-13-a-2003-04-08-43-greece-66313202/542975.html)

   Article: Cook backs push to return Elgin marbles (* to be retrieved from http://www.elginism.com/20040115/marbles-reunited-campaign-launch/)

3. *Benin Bronzes* – It is *originally* from *Nigeria* but now in Glasgow

   News article: Britain's pillaging of the Benin Bronzes begs for a reasonable resolution (* to be retrieved from https://www.theartnewspaper.com/comment/law-restitution-and-the-benin-bronzes)

   News article: Bringing home the Benin Bronzes: Nigeria open to loans rather than a permanent return (* to be retrieved from https://www.telegraph.co.uk/news/2018/06/20/bringing-home-benin-bronzes-nigeria-open-loans-rather-permanent/)

4. *Priam's Gold Collection* – It is *originally* from Troy but *now* in Russia (via Germany)

   News article: Russia refuses to give up Trojan treasure (* to be retrieved from http://www.iol.co.za/scitech/technology/russia-refuses-to-give-up-trojan-treasure-1.235036)

   News Article: Trojan gold fuels rift over war treasures (* to be retrieved from http://www.independent.co.uk/news/world/trojan-gold-fuels-rift-over-war-treasures-1305105.html)

5. *Ancien Marble Head* – carved *head removed* from Anatolia by Britain's consul-general

News article: Turkey demands return of its Elgin marble (* to be retrieved from http://www.independent.co.uk/life-style/history/turkey-demands-return-of-its-elgin-marble-2349791.html)

News article: Echoes of Elgin Marbles: Turkey asks UK to return ancient sculpture (* to be retrieved from http://articles.cnn.com/2011-09-08/world/turkey.archaeological.repatriation_1_anatolia-greek-government-marble-head?_s=PM:WORLD)

Process: Implementation of the Activity

Stage 1

- Students make groups and select an artwork case (or the Teacher decides) to investigate one of the cases regarding misplaced art.
- Students read the informative readings about artworks in order to understand and express the problems related to them. Students look at the roles page to see some suggested questions for the groups.

Stage 2

- Students choose and identify the role of each member in the group.
- Students look at the roles in detail and relevant responsibilities of each member.
- Students talk about the requirements and each person's responsibilities for the final presentation.
- Students wear the name tags to show who you are in the group (Historian, Illustrator, Museum Curator, Lawyer)

Stage 3

Each group member works on her/his share required by her/his role in the group. Each group member tries to answer the questions required because of their roles in the group.

Stage 4

The group members get together in order to prepare for the final presentation to the "Court of Public Opinion." They review the questions required by the roles to check all of the members' progress related to these questions.

Stage 5

Presentation time: The groups do their presentations.

Stage 6

The "Court of Public Opinion" assesses the presentations performed by the groups.

Roles in each team

Historian – person to collect and present the facts about the historical value, background and truth related to the work of art.

Questions to ask

- Who are the involved group of people/countries (stakeholders) related to this work of art?
- What is the historical story of this work of art?
- Where does this piece of art originally come from?
- Where is this piece of art it moved to/take to?
- What is its current situation

Illustrator – person to draw a model, a map, a picture or any form to show the work of art

Questions to ask

- What is this piece of art like?
- What are the physical and visual characteristics of it?
- Where is it now?
- Are there any changes from its original form?

Museum Curator/Appraiser – person to discover and identify the real general facts and figures about the work of art

Questions to ask

- What is this work of art like?
- What is the value of it?
- Where is it now?
- Who possesses this work of art now?

Lawyer – person to search for the law or legal issues related to the work of art

Questions to ask

- Who are the sides that ask for possession of the work of art?
- What does the law say about this issue?
- Whio may hold the legal right to have the possession of the work of art?

Index

affective filter 16
authentic material 16, 20f., 23f., 60f., 72
Chomsky 17
communicative competence 17f., 21
communicative curriculum 18ff.
comprehensible input 15f., 65
course assessment 26, 40, 62, 77
field testing 5, 45, 71f., 78ff.

goals and objectives 20, 25f., 28, 39f., 44
Graves 25f., 41, 43ff., 49-54, 60, 63, 92
instructional foci 66, 68, 77f., 94
Krashen 14ff.
language acquisition 14ff., 52
needs assessment 20f., 25f.
Posner 41, 43f., 53, 77, 93
unit plan 65, 71, 94

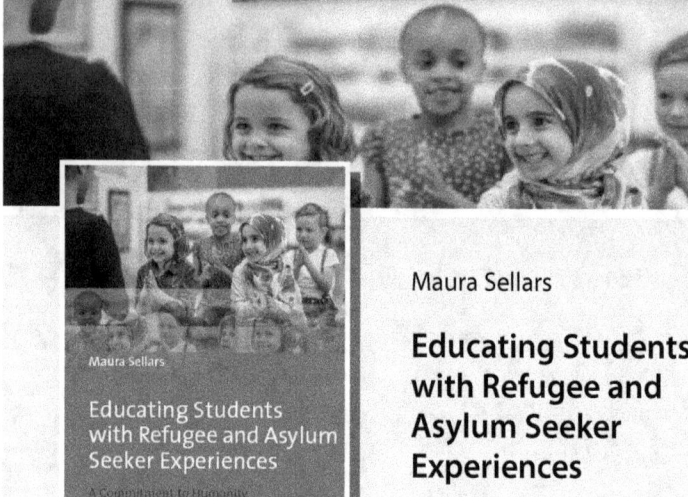

Maura Sellars

Educating Students with Refugee and Asylum Seeker Experiences

A Commitment to Humanity

*2020 • 170 pp. • Pb. • 29,90 € (D) • 30,80 € (A) • ISBN 978-3-8474-2289-1
eISBN 978-3-8474-1313-4 (EPUB) • eISBN 978-3-8474-1345-5 (PDF)*

This book discusses the educational systems into which students with refugee backgrounds are placed when relocated into many of their new homelands. It discusses the current climate of neo liberalism which pervades schooling in many western countries and the subsequent impact on curriculum focus and teaching strategies. It proposes ways in which these students, who are currently the most vulnerable students in school, can be educated with policies and perspectives which respect the diversity and uniqueness that characterises the world today as the result of the global unrest and subsequent diaspora.

www.shop.budrich.de

GPSR Authorized Representative: Easy Access System Europe, Mustamäe tee 50, 10621 Tallinn, Estonia, gpsr.requests@easproject.com

www.ingramcontent.com/pod-product-compliance
Lightning Source LLC
Chambersburg PA
CBHW071146060526
44107CB00133B/331